Rhinoceros

D0770376

Animal
Series editor: Jonathan Burt

Already published

Crow
Boria Sax

Whale
Joe Roman

Ant
Charlotte Sleigh

Parrot
Paul Carter

Tortoise
Peter Young

Tiger
Susie Green

Cockroach
Marion Copeland

Salmon
Peter Coates

Dog
Susan McHugh

Fox
Martin Wallen

Oyster
Rebecca Stott

Fly
Steven Connor

Bear
Robert E. Bieder

Cat
Katharine M. Rogers

Bee
Claire Preston

Peacock
Christine E. Jackson

Rat
Jonathan Burt

Cow
Hannah Velten

Snake
Drake Stutesman

Swan
Peter Young

Falcon
Helen Macdonald

Shark
Dean Crawford

Rhinoceros

Kelly Enright

REAKTION BOOKS

Published by
REAKTION BOOKS LTD
33 Great Sutton Street
London EC1V 0DX, UK
www.reaktionbooks.co.uk

First published 2008
Copyright © Kelly Enright 2008

All rights reserved

No part of this publication may be reproduced, stored in a retrieval
system or transmitted, in any form or by any means, electronic,
mechanical, photocopying, recording or otherwise without the prior
permission of the publishers.

Printed and bound in China

British Library Cataloguing in Publication Data
Enright, Kelly
    Rhinoceros. – (Animal)
    1. Rhinoceroses   2. Animals and civilization
    I. Title
    599.6'68

ISBN-13: 978 1 86189 374 1

Contents

Preface

'Do you know what a rhinoceros looks like?'
'Of course. It's a big, ugly animal.'
Eugène Ionesco, *Rhinoceros* (1959)

Big. Ugly. Violent. Stupid. The rhinoceros has a bad reputation, stretching centuries, even millennia, into our past. When not a villainous symbol of brute force, rhinoceroses are often simply ignored. Although their endangerment in the twentieth and twenty-first centuries has somewhat transformed this image of villainy to one of tragic decline, the heritage of the animals' cultural construction, and its unlikely form, does not garner as much public support as the stars of conservation publicity – the charismatic megafauna – which appeal with the furry cuteness of giant pandas, or the human-like intelligence of gorillas. By contrast, nearly hairless rhinoceroses seem eternally strange. The ways in which we have understood this strangeness is the subject of this book.

I grew up on the New Jersey side of the Hudson River, adjacent to New York City. The rhinos I knew best were the stuffed ones at the American Museum of Natural History. These rhinos were always overshadowed by the more dramatic display at the centre of the Akeley Hall of African Mammals where a startled elephant herd animatedly reacts (it would seem) to the visitors in the museum. I distinctly remember sitting in this dark exhibition space, on the bench which surrounds this mounting, and feeling awed at being so near something so large, so strange, so exotic – and so expressive.

Barnum & Bailey 'Giant Rhinoceros' broadside.

Asian rhinoceros diorama at the American Museum of Natural History, New York.

Also distracting my attention from the rhinos at the far corner of the upper mezzanine were dinosaurs. Even larger and stranger than elephants, mounted dinosaur skeletons were the climax of my museum visit at the impressionable age of six. Little did I realize that the skin I was imagining onto these bones was very like a rhino's skin. Meanwhile, on the other side of Central Park, as I stood in dreamy awe at medieval unicorn tapestries on the wall at the Metropolitan Museum of Art, I did not see the connection between the elegant white horse of mythology and the one-horned pachyderm I so quickly dismissed.

Although rhinoceroses were not an integral piece of my childhood animal cosmology, their cultural history is closely aligned with the elephants, dinosaurs and unicorns that fascinated me. Just as rhinoceroses are difficult to observe in the wild, so are they elusive in cultural spaces. I have not, I admit, met a rhino in the wild. Nor have I had a close encounter with one in captivity. My rhinoceros expedition sought encounters with the wild animal in cultural spaces. After all, this is how most of us know – and have known – the species. Does the non-wildness of my encounters make my knowledge of rhinoceroses less real, less true or less authentic? Perhaps. But it might provide an honest gauge of how humans have related and represented rhinos. What does it mean to see an animal imagined in literature, stuffed in exhibits, browsing behind bars? How do we understand an animal so severed from its native context? Are rhinos more 'themselves' when they are in Asia and Africa? If so, how do we categorize, or separate, the 'real' rhino from the captive, the living being from the creature of the imagination?

The author's close encounter with a rhino (sculpture).

1 Ancient and Mythic

The rhino is a zoological museum piece, a holdover
from times long past, a loner that is unadaptable and
rather stupid.
Edward R. Ricciuti (1980)[1]

One Valentine's Day my boyfriend and I sent each other exactly
the same greeting card. The pink front featured two cartoon
characters – a dinosaur and a unicorn. Bubbles revealed their
forlorn conversation: 'But I'm prehistoric', quipped the
dinosaur, while the unicorn replied, 'And I'm mythological.' The
inside simply read: 'We can work it out.'

If the dinosaur–unicorn romance did 'work out', their offspring would look very much like a rhinoceros. In fact, the rhinoceros has long been associated with these two creatures from
the prehistoric and mythic past.

UNICORNS

Travelling through the region of what is now Sumatra in the
thirteenth century, Marco Polo (1254–1324) reported: 'There
are wild elephants in the country and numerous unicorns
which are very nearly as big.' He described the unicorn as
having the feet of an elephant, the head of a wild boar, and
hair like a buffalo. The horn, he wrote, is placed in the centre
of the forehead and is 'black and very thick'. 'It is a very ugly
beast to look at', Polo continued, 'and is not at all like the one
our stories say is caught in the lap of a virgin. In fact, it is altogether different.'[2]

Confronting a
rhinoceros face
to face.

Stamp seal of the rhinoceros from the Indus Valley.

The familiar creature that inspired Polo to denounce the rhinoceros as an 'ugly beast' was the unicorn – an elegant white horse, with a single long, slender spiralling horn. We know today that the unicorn is an imaginary being. Unlikely as it may seem, the rhinoceros was thought to fulfil all the requirements of the unicorn myth, despite its utterly different anatomy. Here was a creature that eluded capture. Its horn had magical powers; it had a strange tenderness for beautiful virgins; it was unbelievably strong and few had seen it up close.

Unicorn imagery began in South Asia some four thousand years ago. One of the more spectacular unicorn images from the Indus Valley is seen on a stamp that was probably used by a successful merchant to seal a clay tag on his bundles of goods. Other seals from this region depict bulls, elephants and tigers, as symbols of the ruling class. On this seal, we see a creature that seems to be the offspring of a rhinoceros and a unicorn. Its body is heavy and rectangular, like the body of a rhinoceros. Though its horn curves elegantly, like the horn of a unicorn, it has a rhino's ears. Confusion of the two creatures was a good marketing ploy for a merchant trading rhino parts. Perhaps the unicorn lent its magic to horn sold for medicinal purposes.

Images of mythical one-horned creatures circulated through Asian cultures. Some, like the Chinese k'i-lim, resemble dragons, while others look more like horses. But it is an image from mid-sixteenth-century Persia that shows the one-horned creature that most resembles the rhinoceros – the karkadann. The karkadann's origins lie much earlier, and, unlike the gentle k'i-lim, the karkadann was known for its violent nature, and its animosity towards the elephant.

What we know of Asian unicorn mythology comes from Greek naturalists who describe wild asses from India in the fourth century BC. These animals were the size of horses, with

The karkadann, from an 18th-century copy of the *Aja'ib al-Makhluqat* ('Wonders of Creation') by Muhammad al-Qazvini; colour and gold on paper.

white bodies, purple heads and blue eyes. The single horn began as white at the base, changed to black, while the tip was red. The horn was fashioned into cups that were believed to heal and protect those who drank from them. These asses were fast runners. Females could be caught only when caring for young. But even then they could not be captured alive.

Roman writers repeated Greek accounts, but attributed the characteristics of the creature described by Indians to the rhinoceros, not wild asses. The most prominent and permanent descriptions of the unicorn, however, lie in Biblical passages in which the Hebrew word *re'em* is used to describe a one-horned animal with massive muscle. The Greek translation of the Hebrew Bible (second century BC) translates *re'em* as 'monoceros' or single-horned. In the Latin Vulgate Bible, the main version used from 400 through to 1400 CE, re'em, or monoceros was translated to 'unicornis', the Latin word for single horn. As the language of the Church, the Latin word stuck.[3]

The unicorn of the Bible often stands for the power of God. '[H]e hath as it were the strength of a rhinoceros', reveals Numbers, 'he shall eat up the nations his enemies, and shall

The kindred spirits of unicorns and virgins represented in the Unicorn series of tapestries woven in the Netherlands, 1484–1500.

break their bones, and pierce them through with his arrows.' Elsewhere this forcefulness is for good rather than violence: 'His horns are like the horn of the rhinoceros: with them he shall push the people together to the ends of the earth.'

Along with the element of strength, the Bible told of the unicorn's unwillingness to be captured and tamed. 'Will the rhinoceros be willing to serve thee, or abide by thy crib?', reads Job 39:9–11, 'Canst thou bind the rhinoceros with his band in the furrow? Or will he harrow the valleys after thee? Wilt thou trust him, because his strength is great?' As late as the 1830s adventurer R. Gordon Cumming quoted this passage when confronted with a rhinoceros that violently ploughed the ground after being disturbed by the hunter's presence. As will be discussed in the next chapter, rhinoceros and unicorn were similarly conflated when billing them as menagerie attractions. Those who located the unicorn in the rhinoceros were looking for proof of the Bible's accuracy.[4]

Animals mentioned within scriptures were thought by many nineteenth-century naturalists to exist in the physical world; there was no separation of physical and mythological space. With natural history expeditions and the specialization of the field of nature study, there came a similar field of natural theology. Natural theology sought to prove God's existence through studying his creations. The work of observing and cataloguing the natural world was given religious importance.

Natural theologists were determined to prove the Bible was not myth or romance, but natural fact. Previous debates about translations were blamed for much of the confusion of real with mythic creatures. In 1835 Francis A. Ewing, MD, published a guide to teaching the relationship between the biblical and the natural world. His 'Bible Natural History; or a Description of the Animals, Plants, and Minerals, mentioned in the Sacred

A unicorn in a medieval bestiary in the Bodleian Library, Oxford.

Scriptures' highlighted the confusion over the Hebrew translation of 'tannin' and 'tannim'. The first denoted a whale, while the second indicated 'some creature inhabiting the wilderness', which usually referred to owls. Both words, however, came to mean dragon in translation, a misnomer Ewing calls 'worse than meaning'. The similar confusion over *re'em*, unicorn, monoceros, and rhinoceros 'are open to the same objection'. Ewing continued: 'They invest the passages in which they occur with the garb of mythology, and throw a shadow over the authenticity of holy oracles.'

While Ewing discredited the existence of the mythic unicorn, he looked to the tales of travellers who reported various one-horned animals in the Asian wilderness. '[T]here has been found in the deserts of Tibet', he wrote, 'a creature answering in some degree to the one-horned monster of the ancients'. Other accounts aligned it with the narwhal, the oryx or the buffalo. The latter assertion was quickly discredited as buffalo ploughed fields in much of Asia – an activity the unicorn was said to so adamantly resist. '[T]o translate reem by buffalo', observed one missionary who had seen their domestication, 'were to make the Scriptures ridiculous'.[5]

While existing animals did not seem to fit the unicorn bill, more elusive accounts seemingly described the correct creature. In 1821 reports from Asia told of a one-horned animal in the hills east of Nepal. The 'tso'po' was the size of a horse, with cloven hoofs; it was 'fierce and extremely wild' and 'seldom, if ever caught alive'. But to prove one had seen an elusive creature to colleagues thousands of miles away was a task fraught with contradictions. Physical proof of the creature only discredited reports by undermining the animals' elusiveness. Although disembodied horns circulated around Europe, there was no full specimen to prove the shape of the unicorn.[6]

One year after the 'tso'po' account, a Mr Campbell arrived in London bearing a horn attached to a skull from South Africa of 'the Unicorns of ancients, and the same as that which is described in the 39th chapter of the book of Job'. The skull was placed on display at the Museum of the Missionary Society and newspaper accounts of the creature, along with a sketch of the skull, spread across the English-speaking world.

Campbell's accounts of this animal challenged the notion of the 'fancied Unicorn', who is supposed to be the size and shape of a horse. Adding an air of authenticity to his find, Campbell explained that this animal is well known to the native 'Hottentots', who had killed the animal for him. Natives had killed seven rhinoceros in South Africa, he said, but this one

was much larger than the other, 'equal in size to three oxen or four horses'. It behaved like the unicorn described in the Bible; it was 'a very large, ferocious and untamable creature'. Campbell had never seen this animal in the wild and his description of its behaviour was pure conjecture. It was enormous and had a horn; it must be the fierce creature described in biblical accounts.

Although Campbell's skull had a second horn and appeared to be from a rhinoceros, the anterior horn was indeed different than that of a normal rhino; it was longer and straighter, resembling closer that of the heraldic unicorn. Campbell explained away the second horn by saying that from a distance, when the animal is running, only the larger horn would be seen. Thus to

Campbell, the mythic image of the unicorn was a product of the manner in which nature had been previously observed. Those who wrote about a massive one-horned creature were not fabricators of legend, but promoters of an optical illusion. They did not, claimed Campbell, scientifically observe animals by killing and taking specimens, but merely watched from a distance, neither looking for detail nor approaching out of curiosity.

Campbell described his specimen in language meant to counter mythic descriptions. Misled by the Bible, past observers had the creature all wrong. But Campbell's version was hardly a model of scientific accuracy. He had never watched his creature in the wild and he took the skull, along with native accounts of its behaviour, as fact.[7]

Before the nineteenth century, native accounts were folded into biblical description, adding to unicorn mythology another element of the creature's habits – its penchant for beautiful virgins. A tale that originated in India, the first western account appeared in the second-century bestiary *Physiologos*, which tells of an animal the size of a goat who is too quick to be taken alive, though not necessarily because of its violence. Upon encountering a beautiful virgin, it willingly leapt into her lap to be suckled.

Conrad Gesner's unicorn.

Unicornis ein Einhorn.

Unicornis ein Einhorn/ist bei vns ein frembd vnbekandt thier / zim-
licher grösse/doch gegẽ seine treflichen stercke zu rechnen/nit groß von leib/
von farben gelbfarb wie buxbaumen holtz/hat gespalten kloen/wonet im
gebirg vñ bohen wildtnussen/hat vornen an der stirn ein sehr lang scharpff
horn/welches es an den felsen vnd steinen scherpffet,

'[A]bove all other creatures', claimed Conrad Gesner some 1500 years later, 'they love Virgins, and that unto them they will come be they never so wilde, and fall asleep before them, so being asleep, they are easily taken and carried away.'[8]

By the mid-nineteenth century, however, native accounts began to undo the rhino–unicorn confusion. Native accounts were used to identify the real unicorn; inhabitants of Asian and African landscapes were valued as better informed about the animals living within their reaches. Natives from the hills of Nepal were said to bring large spiral horns to the city for trade and 'appear to concur in testimony as to the existence of this animal'. The 'chiro', as they referred to it, was 'too large and fierce to be taken alive'. They collected the horns which had been shed, or from the decaying bodies of dead animals. Such native reports were lent an air of authenticity, in part because they were unaffected by the biblical construction of the unicorn.[9]

Also undoing the mythological ties, nineteenth-century naturalists began to search for more objective 'truths' about nature. 'The researches of modern naturalists are daily confirming the truth of what were once considered the fables of antiquity,' read an 1838 report in the popular newspaper, the *New-York Mirror*. It continued, asserting that the unicorn, 'one of the supporters of the British royal arms, was long supposed to be an invention of the heralds, but has at last been furnished with a "local habitation and a name"'. By attributing to the unicorn a place and name outside biblical language, the rhinoceros was removed from mythic language, replaced by modern, scientific nomenclature.[10]

Once a consensus was reached that the rhinoceros best fit descriptions of the biblical unicorn, the association disappeared. Proof of the biblical unicorn in the form of the rhinoceros did not destroy the myth. It simply rewrote it. As the

Mirror reported, the unicorn was not a biblical but a heraldic image. Certainly, the white horse is a prettier image than the grey, hairless bulk of the rhinoceros, which consequently found a more suitable association with the prehistoric.

PREHISTORIC

While viewing a captive rhinoceros, nineteenth-century naturalist Louis Agassiz was drawn to thoughts of the prehistoric:

> It is remarkable, as proving the changes which our globe has undergone, that this race of animals, which is now confined to tropical regions, has existed in former days in the more temperate and cold districts of Europe, in company with the Elephant and other tropical animals of the present day.[11]

To Agassiz the living rhino stood as a relic of the past. It represented the form of prehistoric animals and inspired imaginings of the ancient landscapes of the western world. The strangeness of the rhinoceros also informed reconstructions of fossil finds. The rhino's association with prehistoric animals engaged it in a dialogue of imagined savage behaviour and inevitable extinction of the 'primitive' in the face of modernity.

Because the chemical consistency of the rhinoceros horn lends itself to the processes of fossilization, it is commonly found among other skeletal remains. When Richard Owen and Benjamin Waterhouse Hawkins constructed a huge model Iguanodon for London's Great Exhibition at Crystal Palace in 1851, they modelled their one-horned dinosaur on the form of a scaly rhinoceros. This half-lizard, half-rhinoceros was the star attraction in the world's first display of sculpted 'prehistoric'

beasts. That this particular horn was actually not a horn at all, but a claw from a completely different specimen, does not discredit the fact that when scientists began imagining the physical appearance of dinosaurs the rhinoceros was top on their list of referential specimens.[12]

The modern naturalist Stephen Jay Gould has described dinosaurs as 'big, fierce, extinct – in other words, alluringly scary, but sufficiently safe'. Extinction, then, was and is understood as a dividing line between the fierce and the tame. This is not to say that all existing nature is harmless, but the nature of the prehistoric past has been imagined as more savage than that of the present. Humans do not have to figure out how to live with, avoid, or control extinct creatures; they can construct their behaviour in any way imaginable, using mythology or science – or both – as their starting point. Thus the unseen nature of the past serves as the ultimate wildness – unknown and unknowable. This temporal distance allows the imagination to run wild with no repercussions from reality – unless of course you are an animal closely resembling those of the prehistoric past. The rhinoceros's unexplainable wildness, its enormity and its rough hairless skin, made it an obvious exemplar of prehistoric life.[13]

As W.J.T. Mitchell argued in his analysis of the cultural meaning of dinosaurs, *The Last Dinosaur Book* (1998), their image 'reflects the fate of nature – and specifically of animals – in the wake of that juggernaut we call "modernity", understood as the whole complex of man-made global forces that is leaving countless extinct species in its wake'. While the rhinoceros's violent behaviour has informed the way we imagine the savage world of dinosaurs, so has the extinction of dinosaurs informed our impressions of rhinoceroses. In the late nineteenth and early twentieth centuries, those who encountered rhinoceroses and saw them as prehistoric also express a sense of inevitability

'The Extinct Animal' room at the Crystal Palace included B. W. Hawkins's Iguanodon, seen here surrounded by other dinosaurs in Hawkins's workshop.

Dish with
mounted hunters
and animals from
8th-century
Vietnam.

to their extinction. Tangled in a web of modernity and endangerment, the rhinoceros was perceived as unfit to survive in the modern era.[14]

'Like men of the old stone age', wrote naturalist-hunter Herbert Lang in 1920, 'with but few implements for defense or attack compared with the multitude of destructive weapons in our times, the rhinoceros seems to lag ages behind in the development of its various senses.' The rhinoceros's inability to adapt to human technology, Lang wrote, leaves it 'hopelessly doomed by modern firearms'. What now seems a tragic irony – hunters shooting an animal they recognize they are implicit in endangering – to them looked not like irony, but the inevitability of 'progress'. After killing his share of rhinoceroses, President-adventurer Theodore Roosevelt paused to observe one at rest.

'Look at him', reflected his son, Kermit, 'standing there in the middle of the African plain, deep in prehistoric thought.' The elder Roosevelt agreed: 'Indeed the rhinoceros does seem like a survival from the elder world that has vanished; he was in place in the Pliocene; he would not have

24

been out of place in the Miocene; but nowadays he can only exist at all in regions that have lagged behind, while the rest of the world, for good or for evil, has gone forward.'[15]

Over a century earlier, the existence of fossil rhinoceros finds invoked a sense of national pride for two reasons. Akin to Roosevelt's reflections on the animal, the fact that rhinoceroses no longer existed on American soil implied the nation was progressing. While the regions still containing rhinoceroses had, as Roosevelt asserted, 'lagged behind'. The second push to publicize rhinoceros finds involved their size.

During the eighteenth century, large fossilized bones were found throughout the eastern United States, inspiring dreams of giant beasts that might still exist in the unexplored west. Sending the first expedition, in 1802, President Thomas Jefferson (himself an excavator of fossils) explicitly told the explorers Lewis and Clark to look for living mammoths. More than mere curiosity was behind the president's desire to discover this enormous animal living on the American continent. French naturalist Georges-Louis Leclerc, Comte de Buffon (1707–1788), had asserted that American wildlife was diminutive and degenerate in comparison with that of the Old World. National pride was at stake in locating impressive animal specimens. While no living 'monsters' were found, fossil finds continued to play into American conceptions of their nation's 'wildness' – even if that wildness was in the past.

Historian Paul Semonin convincingly argued in his *American Monster* (2000) that the '[b]elief in the savagery of prehistoric nature . . . had its roots in the master metaphor of early American national culture – the myth of wild nature, the idea that the New World was a wilderness inhabited by savages.' Proving America had large, ferocious, wild animals – even if

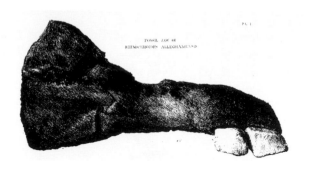

FOSSIL JAW OF
RHINOCEROIDES ALLEGHANIENSIS

they no longer existed – was key to the young nation's sense of
self. Semonin located in the mammoth the first articulation of
this paradigm that 'transformed a herbivorous, elephant-like
creature into the terror of the antediluvian world'. Like its associations with dinosaurs, rhinoceros fossils from America's Ice
Age inspired images of ferocity that boosted the ego of
Americans while placing on the rhinoceros the weight of imagined prehistoric savagery.[16]

In 1831 G. W. Featherstonehaugh wrote confidently that
he had found the fossil jaw of 'an extinct animal', a possible
ancestor of the rhinoceros, in the Allegheny Mountains of
Pennsylvania. After comparing the fossil jaw to that of a
modern rhinoceros skeleton, he wrote: 'Unwilling to designate
it by any fanciful or philonymic appellation, and thinking
that by some naturalists it may be judged to stand in the same
relation to the genus rhinoceros, that the elephant does to the
mastodon, I have provisionally named it Rhinoceroides
Alleghaniensis.'[17]

Featherstonehaugh's discovery of *R. Alleghaniensis* gave
America a native representative of this prehistoric beast, named
for the mountains in which its remains were found. The naming
was an act of claiming this beast for the nation, forever tying its

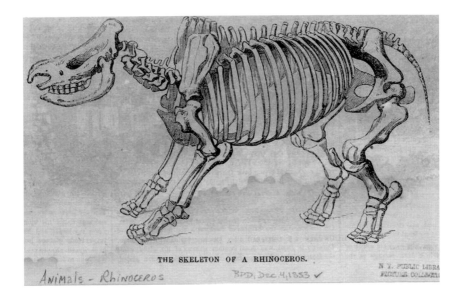

THE SKELETON OF A RHINOCEROS.

Animals - Rhinoceros   BPD, Dec 4, 1853 ✓   N. Y. PUBLIC LIBRA
PICTURE COLLECTI

form with the region of its discovery. Despite its long absence from the continent, rhino bones played a part in reconstructing the ancient wildness of American nature.

In the same year of Featherstonehaugh's discovery the first living rhinoceros arrived in Boston Harbor. Advertising for this Indian rhinoceros employed both the associations of the prehistoric and its alignment with the mythic unicorn. Thus its behaviour was perceived as doubly wild. 'The Rhinoceros, or Unicorn', as it was billed, 'is not numerous, and he is rarely taken alive, but never without much hazard.' The act, then, of capturing a rhinoceros was a feat in and of itself; the rhino was worth seeing for its rarity, and for the wonder of gazing upon an animal so difficult to take alive. In the ads and articles regarding this rhinoceros, there is no debate about whether or not it was a unicorn. A few use the phrase 'supposed to be the unicorn

An early sketch of rhinoceros bones.

27

from scripture' but none explicitly deny the relation. Thus, in the popular imagination, if not for certain in scientific or biblical nomenclature, the rhinoceros *was* the unicorn. Thus the rhinoceros in America was a living symbol of human dominance over even the most wild of creatures.[18]

Likewise, the captive rhinoceros stood as a relic of the prehistoric landscape of America. As Agassiz reflected upon the relation of the existing animal to its fossil remains he, like many others, imagined a sublime wildness upon the living creature which seemed a leftover from a more savage age. Visitors to the rhinoceros saw more than a representative from another land, but a former inhabitant of the imagined landscape of prehistoric America. As the next chapter explores, captive rhinoceroses made significant contributions to understanding rhino behaviour, but they were not immune to these former associations. Unicorn mythology and imaginings of the prehistoric haunted constructions of rhinoceros character, even as living specimens disproved the species' reputation for ferocity.

2 Rhinos on the Road

'[T]he rhinoceros maintained its characteristic ugliness.'
Phoebe George Bradford,
a visitor to the Boston rhinoceros, 1934[1]

'In the same solemnities of *Pompey*, as many times else', wrote Greek naturalist Pliny the Elder (AD 23 79), 'was shewed a Rhinoceros, with one horne and no more, and the same in his snout or muzzle'. When Pliny completed his *Natural History* (c. AD 77) he was among the first westerners to describe rhinoceroses with the benefit of first-hand observation.

When Philadelphos ruled in Egypt, he imported scores of exotic animals to Alexandria. In 275–274 BC, he paraded animals through the streets of that city to celebrate a holiday he created, the Ptolemaia – a once every four year celebration in honour of his father (Ptolemy), Alexander the Great, and the Olympian gods. In a reenactment of wine-god Dionysos' supposed victorious return from India, a five-and-a-half-metre statue of the god was wheeled ahead of nearly a hundred elephants drawing chariots. Other animals were doing the same – oryx, goats, saiga antelopes, swift hartebeests, ostriches. At the end of the parade, men led a white bear, fourteen leopards, nine cheetahs, four caracals, a giraffe and a white rhinoceros from Ethiopia.[2]

For Philadelphos the rhinoceros was an exotic symbol of his empire. Unlike his scores of elephants, it was not a useful beast, but a representative of lands he had explored, conquered, and held tame. For centuries western culture would acquire similar menageries. Captive animals have multiple meanings to the people who keep and view them. The rhinoceros is ever a rarity. This chapter explores a few famous captive rhinoceroses – and the thoughts, science and art they inspired.

Greek audiences were long familiar with elephants and Pliny took the fellow pachyderm as his point of comparison when he viewed the rhino. While the skin and build is similar, he said, there is nothing in the natural world more opposed than their natures. The elephant was 'the greatest, and commeth nearest in wit and capacitie, to men', he wrote, explaining that it understands languages and commands, is easily trained, and 'take[s] a pleasure and delight both in love and also in glorie'.

In contrast, Pliny's rhinoceros was either not willing or too boorish to be trained, and 'is a second enemie by nature to the Elephant'. 'He fileth that horne of his against hard stones', claimed Pliny, 'and maketh it sharpe against he should fight.' When matched with the elephant, the rhinoceros 'layeth principally at his bellie, which he knoweth to be more tender than the rest'. Plotting, conniving and underhanded (or underhorned), Pliny's perception of the rhinoceros was not a flattering one. If the elephant was a noble creature akin to Greek men, it seems the rhinoceros represented the savagery of their unenlightened enemies.[3]

Pliny did not describe actually observing this supposed battle of elephant and rhino. The origins of the rivalry seem to lie in a Persian myth that told of the one-horned Karkadann. Feared by all other animals, this creature lived in isolation. The elephant, not having yet heard of the Karkadann's bad temper, approached him. When the two animals first set eyes on each other, there arose an instant instinctual hatred.

کند و بمیرد و آنکه روز کار در از اژدها و خه کند و بچه کنند تا بچه دیگر برآید و بچه در شکم مادر سپ
از فرج مادر بیرون کند و مادرش طعام می دهد و جای بی از میشود جانورست
مملکت بهایم ما ندبی سنج و سرو دنبال که و سباع مانند که دست و پای
شیر دارد و کردن اسب و یک سرو دار و محکم از پیشانی وی برآمده و با

ملک نیست

پیل در آویزد و پیل را بپرو بردارد و با فیل عداوت دارد جنگ کنند
و سروی دار و معقف درشت فیل آویزد میجان مانند تا هر دو هلاک
شوند و کرکدن از عمر ان دور باشد و حدث وی سوزنده دارست و کویند

The karkadann spearing an elephant in a Persian copy of the *Aja'ib al-Makhluqa*t ('Wonders of Creation') of c. 1550.

As the tale continued, the elephant flapped its ears and bellowed from its trunk while the karkadann stomped the ground and rubbed its horn on a nearby rock. The two animals charged towards each other. As the elephant's tusks moved towards the karkadann, it ducked. Surprised by this move, the elephant reared on its hind legs, leaving its stomach vulnerable. The karkadann took advantage and pierced it with its horn. Mortally wounded, the elephant fell upon the ground on top of its killer. Weakened from thrashing about trying to get free, and blinded by elephant blood and fat dripping into its eyes, the karkadann gave up and lay down. Just then a huge bird swooped down and lifted the two creatures together, placing them in her nest where her babies fed on their flesh.[4]

In ancient Rome five days of animal shows were held in the Circus Maximus. Hundreds of thousands gathered to look down upon artificially rendered landscapes within the stadium consisting of hills, streams and forests in which man and beast

Peter Kolb, *The Rhinoceros (after Dürer) Fighting an Elephant* (1745).

were set loose. Along with lions and leopards, rhinoceroses were viewed, impressing all with their 'noble demise'. Having heard tales of the elephant–rhino duel, they matched the two in battle, but it seems nothing happened – or at least nothing worth preserving in the written record.[5]

Although the Greeks and Romans held captive rhinoceroses, from the third to the sixteenth centuries not a single rhino came to Europe. Elephants had been continually bred in captivity since Roman times, leaving a line of captives in European menageries; but rhinoceroses had completely disappeared from European soil. The rigours of the sea journey, compounded with the overland trek by horse-drawn carriage, left the rhino one of the most mysterious of mammals.

When a rhinoceros was imported for the first time in over a millennium one of the first desires of its owners was to test the supposed elephant–rhino animosity. As a gift, Muzafar II, ruler of Gujarat in India, had sent an Indian rhinoceros to Alfonso d'Albuquerque (the governor of Portugal's Indian territories), who then presented it to his superior, King Manuel. On 3 June 1515 the king set the rhinoceros and an elephant loose in a ring in Lisbon. In the dullest of anticlimaxes, both animals avoided each other, wandering to opposite ends of the arena.

Although there is no mention of another attempt to exhibit the elephant–rhino rivalry, a rhinoceros that arrived in Portugal in 1577, at the court of Philip II, was exhibited with great success alongside an elephant. This Indian rhinoceros was apparently quite violent. It killed one keeper and, when the others could not control it, they shaved its horn down. It was nearly or wholly blind, and may have been intentionally deprived of sight by its keepers. When it died in 1603, although its skin was not well preserved, its horn and bones were sent to emperor Rudolf – who had sought the living rhino for his extensive menagerie. Rudolf

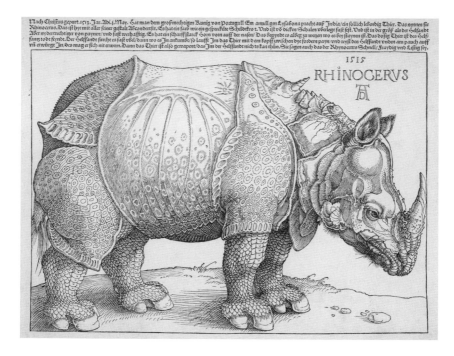

Nach Christus gepurt.1513. Jar.Adi.1.May. Hat man dem grofimechtigen Kunig von Portugall Emanuel gen Lysabona pracht auß India/ein sollich lebendig Thier. Das nennen sie Rhinocerus.Das ist hye mit aller seiner gestalt Abcondertsit.Es hat ein farb wie ein gespreckelte Schildtkro t. Vnd ist vo dicken Schalen vberlegt fast fest. Vnd ist in der gröf als der Helfandt Aber nydertrechtiger von paynen/ vnd fast werh afftig. Es hat ein scharff starck Horn vorn auff der nasen/ Das beginndt es allheg zu wetzen wo es bey staynen ist.Das dosig Thier ist des Helfi sants todt feyndt.Der Helfandt furchts es fast vbel/dann wo es Jn ankumbt/so laufft Jm das Thier mit dem kopff zwischen dye fordern payn/vnd reyst den Helfandt vndem am pauch auff vn erwürgt Jn.des mag er sich nit erwam.Dann das Thier ist also gewapent/das Jm der Helfande nicht ts kan thun.Sie sagen auch das der Rhynocerus Schnell/ Fraydig vnd Lustig sey.

1515

RHINOCERVS

Albrecht Dürer,
Rhinoceros (1515).

had objects from his Kunstkammer (cabinet of curiosity, the earliest form of museum) illustrated in a book, the *Museum of Rudolf II* – including the rhinoceros horn.[6]

Whether out of disappointment at the rhino's sedateness, or simply out of respect for his spiritual leader, when the elephant–rhino duel fell through King Manuel sent the rhinoceros to Pope Leo X in Rome. It boarded the ship decorated in roses and carnations, wearing a jewelled collar and gilt-iron chain. This adornment may take the credit for the most long-standing misconception about rhinoceros physiognomy in history.

Not having seen the animal himself, Albrecht Dürer (1471–1528) sketched a beast with three horns and bumps all over its

heavily armoured skin. His creation, *Rhinoceros* (1515), became the most common image of a rhinoceros in Europe for two hundred years afterwards. It was compiled from the description of someone who had seen the rhinoceros in Lisbon that same year, as it was adorned to board the ship. There is some evidence that the Lisbon rhinoceros might have worn armour, which was part of Muzafar's original gift. While the Indian rhinoceros has only one horn, some interpret Dürer's dorsal horn as the pommel of an Indian saddle. Seemingly dressed for battle, the Lisbon rhinoceros was bombed with oranges in a mock battle as the ship docked in Marseilles.

Despite Dürer not having set eyes upon a living or even dead rhinoceros, his sketch stood in western culture as the most influential of rhino images. For centuries Europeans would copy his work when depicting the species. The heavily plated, armoured look of the rhino's skin enforced the image of the rhino as fierce warrior, as Pliny had described it a thousand years earlier.[7]

Dürer's armour-clad rhinoceros enforced the image of rhino as warrior for over two centuries. A specimen in London in 1684, whose plated skin was likened to 'the Wings of a Dragon', was said to toss any object thrown at it into the air, 'or else bores it through, whether Iron or Stone'. Although not personally witnessed by the writer, he described the rhinoceros's 'Natural Antipathy' for the elephant, and its stabbing of the elephant's belly 'and so ripping open his Gutts'.[8]

Not until the mid-eighteenth century did a rhinoceros appear to inspire new images which would somewhat lessen the rhino's ferocious reputation. As historian Glynis Ridley related in her tale of this animal's tour of Europe, *Clara's Grand Tour* (2004), the correction of Dürer's skewed image of the rhinoceros in European culture is owed to a single specimen of Indian rhinoceros – Clara.

A German broadside advertising Van der Meer and Clara.

Dutch sea captain Douwemout van der Meer acquired the Indian rhinoceros as a baby. Since it was a small animal, his first challenge was not capturing it or keeping it under control, but simply keeping it alive at sea. He kept her hide hydrated with fish oil. Having survived the journey to Leiden, Clara and Van der Meer embarked on a land tour in which they crossed the Rhine River, paused at Louis xv's menagerie at Versailles, and arrived at the court of Empress Maria Theresa in Vienna.

Clara's travels, argues Ridley, 'presents a strong claim as one of the first recognizably modern media campaigns'. There were broadsides, promotional literature, souvenirs – all created to titillate audiences before she arrived and/or to leave mementos of the experience when she left. If eighteenth-century audiences did not know they wished to see a rhinoceros, Clara's handler told them why they must.[9]

For most Europeans, seeing Clara was a chance to know an exotic animal first hand, to personally observe and testify to the rhinoceros's form and behaviour. It was also an event that inspired and called upon the fashion for the exotic. Advertisements for Clara juxtaposed her with palm trees and African natives with bows and arrows, enforcing her exoticness. In true 'orientalist' fashion, the rhinoceros from India was imagined with natives of countries to which it had no association, even Native Americans. Geographic context didn't matter, only the implication of the exotic. In one anonymous Venetian painting Clara was paired with the two-and-a-half-metre Irish giant Magrath – a testament both to her bulk and to her rarity.[10]

The rhinoceros was so unfamiliar, so exotic, that Casanova joked in his diary that, upon taking a lady to see Clara at the St Germain Fair in Paris, she approached the dark man in African dress who was collecting admission fees inquiring if *he* was the rhinoceros. Pietro Longhi's painting portrayed visitors in

Clara inspired souvenirs and artworks, including this French clock.

Venice going to see Clara in disguise. Going to see Clara was an act of appreciation of the exotic, as well as the observation of a much-mythologized animal. One image has Clara in the foreground while in a desert background a rhino is goring an elephant with its horn, playing out the long-standing myth of these animals' animosity.

The famous, the aristocratic and the royal went to see the rhinoceros and continued to relate to its image by including it in their own images. The granddaughter of Louis xv is painted in the portrait *Maria Luisa of Bourbon-Parma* (1765) by Laurent Pecheux (Palazzo Pitti, Florence), accompanied by a Clara-inspired clock resting on a nearby table. Jean-Etienne Liotard's small portrait of Archduke Karl Joseph showed him sitting with a book open to the page inscribed 'Le Rhinoceros', on which is shown an illustration of an Indian rhinoceros. Seeing the rhinoceros and owning a piece of rhino memorabilia was a symbol of high society.[11]

Pietro Longhi's rendering of spectators viewing Clara shows the event as a masquerade, 1751.

In France, Clara became more than a testament to the reality of rhinoceros-ness – she inspired what historian Louise E. Robbins called a 'veritable "rhinomania"'. Rhino imagery was found in poems, hairstyles ('coiffures à la rhinocéros'), engravings and clock bases. While rhinos were featured on clocks in Germany as well, they had used the same model, while the French employed four different poses. One showed the rhino bellowing, revealing a little-portrayed animated and slightly aggressive Clara. Some rhino clocks had music and movement. One featured a Native American figure with bow and arrow.[12]

The rhinoceros craze influenced not just art and artefact, but fashion. Feathers and ribbons wound up in hairstyles represented the rhinoceros horn and tail, respectively. Together, these two items symbolized promiscuity in French culture, and at least one woman snuck her lover into her house disguised as a cardboard rhinoceros. Either the French simply found the form of the rhinoceros erotic, which with its erect horn is not a giant stretch of the imagination, or they had heard of its sexual encounters in the wild, where the males of the species are known to ejaculate repeatedly over the course of an hour's intercourse. Although this information was not used to officially market Clara, nor does it appear in contemporary natural histories, the association with other promiscuous items implies the rhinoceros was not just exotic, but erotic.[13]

It would indeed have been difficult to observe anything about rhinoceros sex life through this single, young specimen. What visitors did observe in Clara's behaviour would seem to be enough to disprove tales of unrelenting violence. This was not the case. The single specimen was not enough, it seems, to rewrite the more generalized image of the rhinoceros and its habits en masse. While Clara's advertising described her as exotic and naturally fierce, her gentle behaviour was observed

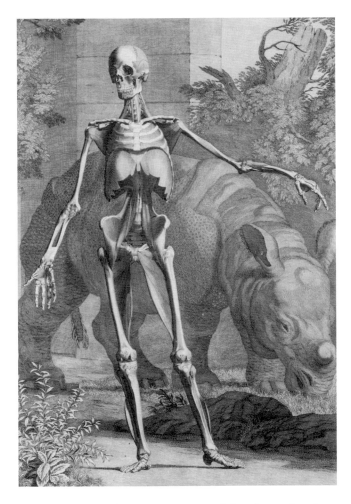

Albinus and Wanderlaar's publication used Clara as a scale model to set beside a human skeleton.

by more than one observer. One reported that she was 'gentle as a dove' and was allowed to roam free like a pet dog. Clara would cross the room to retrieve her favourite treats of beer, tobacco and oranges. This seems to the be the only 'trick' Van der Meer taught Clara, though she was overall a docile animal, and was even observed licking her keeper's face.

In contrast to portrayals of her exoticness, the Northumberland Meissen service of porcelain dishes featured Clara at the centre of a platter with flowers and insects. Delicate and realistic, the rhino is not armoured for warfare, or drawn with exotic objects. Instead, she is associating serenely with the smallest and most delicate of natural things. In a reference to Dürer, the artist placed a flower in the spot where his inaccurate (or misunderstood) dorsal horn had been. Other pastoral imaginings of Clara circulated widely. Johann Elias Ridinger's portrayal of Clara at rest, *The Dutch Rhinoceros Lying on its Left Side* (1748), and Longhi's depiction of the close proximity of rhino to visitors speak to Clara's docility. While Clara did serve to reconstruct the mistaken image of rhinoceros form, she seems to have failed in conveying a new understanding of rhinoceros behaviour at large.[14]

Those who seemed most inclined to take Clara's behaviour as evidence of rhinoceros character were naturalists. Clara provided a unique opportunity to observe the wild animal up close, inspiring the work of some of the era's most influential natural history texts. In his *Histoire Naturelle* Georges-Louis Leclerc published an illustration of a cumbersome rhinoceros, bearing a delicate horn. This image was based on a life-size portrait of Clara painted by Jean-Baptiste Oudry in 1749. The illustration placed the rhinoceros against the backdrop of a seemingly natural habitat, precariously perched on a cliff surrounded by grassy earth and mountains. Unlike the portrayals of Clara discussed above, the rhinoceros was not set against the context of exotic amusement, but imagined back in the wild.[15]

Removed from the menagerie, Clara became simply a rhinoceros, a representative of her species. Although this picture is based on

Clara, Buffon does not indicate the identity of the rhinoceros in his text. By invoking not amusement, fashion, exotica, or erotica, Buffon's rhino conjured the sublime in nature. Additionally, Buffon's rhino looks directly at the viewer. It is not a specimen distanced from the viewer's experience, but looking, addressing, engaging, even confronting the viewer of the illustration.

The returned gaze of Buffon's rhinoceros indicates recognition of the animal's awareness (if not intelligence), and the possibility of a relationship between human and rhino. In his *An History of the Earth and Animated Nature* (1774), Oliver Goldsmith followed his ancient predecessor Pliny in placing the entry for rhinoceros directly after elephant. Goldsmith's account of the rhinoceros, however, employed a different type of observation of the living animal than did Pliny's. He was able to watch Clara closely for an extended time as she interacted with viewers and her handler.

'Next to the elephant, the rhinoceros is the most powerful of animals', wrote Goldsmith, '[b]ut though the rhinoceros is thus formidable by nature, yet imagination has not failed to exert itself, in adding to its terrors.' Looking at Clara did not measure up to other reports Goldsmith had read or heard of rhino behaviour. 'I have often seen it lick a young man's face who kept it', he explained, 'and both seemed pleased with the action'. For Goldsmith, this remarkable act of gentleness undermined the myth of rhinoceros ferocity.

Goldsmith used his observations to thoroughly disprove another myth about the rhinoceros. It was said that in addition to consorting with tigers, when a rhinoceros killed a human, 'it continues to lick the flesh quite from the bone with its tongue, which is said to be extremely rough'. This story was reported by Marco Polo (1254–1324) in the thirteenth century, as he wrote that his 'unicorns' 'do no harm with the horn, however, but only

A rhinoceros illustrated in Goldsmith's *An History of the Earth and Animated Nature* (1774).

with the tongue, for this is covered with long hard thorns and when the unicorns are angry they hold their victim under their knees and grate him . . .'. With the advantage of closer examination, Goldsmith compared the rhino tongue to the smoothness of velvet. Furthermore, he asserted that rhinos and tigers do not 'consort' together, but are seen together only 'because they both frequent watery places in the burning climates where they are bred'. Such stories, asserted Goldsmith, are 'fabulous'.[16]

Into the nineteenth century naturalists continued to tame the rhinoceros's wildness. Observing other captive rhinoceroses after Clara's death, Georges Cuvier (1769–1832) and Carl Joseph Brodtmann (1787–1862) follow Buffon in their romantic depictions of rhinoceros sublimity. Cuvier accompanied his text with an illustration of a rhino in a marsh around a lake. Its physical form is more naturalistic than most, with smoother skin and seemingly accurate depiction of the horn. Cuvier's rhino is not standing frozen in time and space, but seems occupied by its own life. Brodtmann's two lithographs of the Indian rhinoceros

in *The Natural History of Mammals* (1827) showed the animal standing on a tuft of grass, head down and eyes on the ground. Though less romantic an image than Cuvier's, Brodtmann's recognized the rhino's life as something apart from the human. By thus removing the rhinoceros from its known context as an amusement, naturalists who recognized the docility of captive rhino behaviour as possibly reflective of free rhinos, also reimagined its wildness. Perhaps not as violent as the unicorn or prehistoric associations had previously constructed, the rhinoceros was represented here as sublimely 'other'.

'PAROXYSMS OF RAGE': THE BOSTON RHINOCEROS

In 1855 a rhino named Old Put gave a wholly new impression of captive rhinos. This specimen deigned to do tricks. Showman Dan Rice (1823–1900) trained it to sit, lie down, grunt, walk slow and fast and up steps. Its best circus trick was to ring a fire bell in a skit. Even this, however, did not impress discerning audiences looking for real entertainment and used to animals that could do much more. Old Put was 'unanimously voted a humbug and a bore'.[17]

Although the presence of a rhinoceros in a circus act would seemingly disprove its penchant for violence, the significance of Old Put to nineteenth-century audiences had more to do with man than with animal. Old Put had reportedly killed a previous owner, and Rice's bravery in taking on the animal seemed to be tempting fate. Indeed, the rhino did stab Rice once, sending him to the hospital for several days. While Old Put was a bore, Rice was praised for having 'exercised his will over "the most obdurate disposition of animal nature"'.

This sort of wildness has nothing to do with setting. Throughout the nineteenth century, the public image of the rhinoceros implied that while you can take the rhino out of the wilderness, you cannot take the wildness out of the rhinoceros. When the first living specimen set foot on American shores in 1830, its

THE UNICORN.

A rhinoceros headlining a mid-19th-century menagerie advert, and billed as 'THE UNICORN'.

Brodtmann's Indian rhinoceros.

An Indian
rhinoceros
engaged in
a'paroxysm
of rage'.

promoters spotlighted its 'paroxysms of rage' to market their
attraction. An advertisement in the *Saturday Evening Post*
described the behavior of the Boston rhinoceros:

> He possesses surprising strength, is totally untractable,
> and subject to paroxysms of fury which nothing can
> appease. With the horn o[n] his nose, he tears up trees,
> raises up heavy stones, and throws them behind him to a
> considerable distance.[18]

Another claimed that while it is 'not of a ferocious nature', it 'is
sometimes liable to paroxysms of rage'. Accompanying this

GREAT INDIAN RHINOCEROS IN THE ZOOLOGICAL GARDENS.

colourful description is an illustration of the rhinoceros stand-ing in profile without emotion or evidence of such intractable behavior, seemingly contradicting the description. Like Clara before her, the first rhino in America bore the weight of more than a millennium's worth of mythology.

Billed as the 'unicorn from scripture', the act of going to see the Boston rhinoceros was a testament to its biblical origins and the increasing knowledge of the natural world. This rhino was

Lydekker's Great Indian Rhinoceros in its enclosure.

also representative of non-western places, and associated with the romantic and exotic. Ads told of its capture 'at the foot of one of the Himalay mountains, near a branch of the Ganges'. Before coming to the States, it was owned by 'a Rajah or native Prince in Calcutta'. The ad makes a more dubious claim that Indian and African natives eat its 'much relished' flesh. An article on the natural history of the rhinoceros published upon the rhino's arrival invoked the ancient calling it a 'great rarity . . . that was better known to the ancients, since we have accounts of him from Pliny, Dion, Cassius . . .'. It continued, by explaining the rhino's violence through Pliny's assertions, not through the writer's personal observations.[19]

The writer does offer some of his own observations of the display of the Boston rhinoceros – though they are not flattering. 'The animal now with us', he continued, 'appears to be of a stupid nature, and exhibits no traits of intelligence or instinct beyond those of the Hog, to which he seems to be allied in manners as well as form'. After asserting the peacefulness of the rhino, he continued with description of the animal's dumbness. It 'appears to distinguish no one around him, and to be insensible to every thing but the calls of appetite'. 'It is singular', he continued:

> that his natural placidity of temper should be interrupt-
> ed by a fit of passion, which he is subject to every day,
> with the greatest regularity, and sometimes twice a day.
> The fury attacks h[i]m, with more or less of violence,
> during which he is entirely ungovernable, runs about
> butting with his horn against any thing within his reach,
> and is only appeased by offering him some of his favorite
> sweet food.[20]

The unexplainable 'paroxysms of rage' appear to be simply a desire for food, though the writer does not make this association explicit.

Despite such observations, the lethal combination of mythic heritage and forbidding appearance was difficult to overcome. Nineteenth-century audiences seemed convinced of the ferocity of rhinoceroses. In 1873 a writer for *Appleton's Journal* asserted that the rhino, not the lion, was 'king of the beasts'. It 'is certainly more dangerous, and . . . could kill him in a few moments'.[21]

'GIANT PETS': BESSIE

Because of the rhinoceros's heritage of violence, when Colonel Pollack reported accounts of twelve tame rhinoceroses in the court of an Indian ruler many found it difficult to believe. An equally astounding report was of a rhinoceros so tame it carried loads of laundry on its back for its keeper. An English journalist told a tale of a semi-tame rhinoceros in the London menagerie at Exeter Change upon whose back rode the eighteenth-century actor 'the great John Philip Kemble' who had 'borrowed of Mr. Crosse the Rhinoceros on which he took his ever-memorable ride through Covent Garden Market – in the early morning, when the sun was bright, and saloop-stalls were yet about – as dignified as a lord, playing the fool as only wise men can.'

It is difficult to tell whether Kemble's rhinoceros ride made the man more wild or the beast more tame. But the same journalist, writing at least thirty years after this supposed event, associated Kemble, famous for his portrayal of Macbeth, and the rhinoceros with Shakespeare's brief reference to the animal as a 'Hyrcanian beast' in that play. In imagining the scene at Exeter Change, the journalist heard 'the howlings of unnumbered savage brutes, the rugged Russian bear, the armed rhinoceros, like the Hyrcanian beast, shook the bricks'. Real evidence of rhinoceros rage existed right in the same city. Over at the London Zoo a rhinoceros with the unassuming name Jim nearly killed his keeper until the keeper of the famous elephant Jumbo hit him in the eye. After this attack, Jim remained at the zoo and lived out an apparently otherwise non-violent life, at forty years possibly the longest of any rhino kept in captivity.[22]

Such evidence of tameness did not replace imaginings of the wild, however, until the twentieth century, when the reputation of rhinoceroses gradually became less maligned. The dawn of the modern zoo and extensive scientific observations of their behavior informed new impressions, cutting the centuries-long process of reinforcing and reshaping rhinoceros mythology.

An elephant and rhino meet in their enclosures at the Bronx Zoo.

Thus when the Bronx Zoo obtained a baby black rhinoceros in 1906 New York Zoological Society president Elwin Sanborn described it as 'bright and energetic, and entirely satisfactory as an exhibit'.[23]

The black rhino was the most expensive animal yet obtained by the zoo, also in possession of an Indian rhinoceros, known by the name Mogul. The black rhino was obtained in Mombasa, East Africa, by biologist and hunter Herbert Lang. Despite his negative portrayal of adult rhinos in his hunting essays (to be discussed in the next chapter), Lang reported that this specimen's 'monstrous weight and power is not so serious a drawback'. The young, he said, are 'giant pets' which 'show great affection for those attending them and at the slightest call give instant response'.[24]

These valuable exhibits did not come without complications. When Mogul developed visible eye problems, surgery was performed on him in 1908. 'Since we always prided ourselves on the fine physical condition of our specimens', wrote curator Raymond Ditmars, Mogul's poor health was 'a serious drawback to his exhibition value'. Administering a pound and a half of chloroform and three quarter pounds of ether, sedating the rhino was no easy task, but necessary, as Ditmars joked, since '[t]here was no possibility of fitting Mogul out with glasses'.[25]

Mogul regained full sight in his left eye, but had only partial sight in his right, which keepers thought he had injured in the wild. Sanborn called his death in 1918 'the greatest loss in [the zoo's] history, thus far'. At the time Mogul was only one of three rhinos known in captivity. In 1906 the zoo paid $6,000 for it; when it died its value had appreciated to $25,000. Its skin and skeleton were given to the American Museum of Natural History.[26]

Such valuable attractions were soon given an equally impressive home. Completed in 1908, the Elephant House was,

Berlin Zoo's
Pachyderm House
in the 1860s.

wrote William Temple Hornaday, president of the New York
Zoological Society, 'the crowning feature of the Zoological
Park'. '[S]pacious, beautifully designed, well built, perfectly
lighted, heated and ventilated', the new building was not only
an architectural gem, but a pleasing environment for its residents. Open-air yards were attached to the indoor areas, which
were over 7 metres square and lit by skylight.

'We are extremely fortunate', continued Hornaday, 'in being
able to exhibit a collection of elephants and rhinoceroses in every
way worthy of the new building.' The building's initial residents
included two rhinoceroses and two hippos along the north side.
The south side was residence to four elephants. Hornaday gladly
reported that all these animals 'greatly enjoy their fine quarters'.[27]

Detail of a rhinoceros on Bronx Zoo's Elephant House, sculpted by A. Phimister Proctor.

The Elephant House's exterior reflected the animals housed inside. Arch entrances are flanked by sculpted stone elephant heads with a single rhinoceros head at the apex of the archway. On the south side of the building these represent Indian animals, and were carved by A. Phimister Proctor, while on the north side Charles R. Knight sculpted specimens from Africa. The realism of the work of these two artists was part of the building's attraction. '[T]hese are fine examples of wild-animal sculpture', Hornaday wrote, 'and well illustrate the extent to which the realism of Nature may be fitly applied to a modern building, in place of the grotesque and conventionalized sculptures that hitherto have enjoyed the favor of architects'. Along the cornice are heads of rhino, tapir and hippopotamus. Inside the building, columns which separate cages are adorned with elephant heads.[28]

With a somewhat heavy hand, Hornaday assured visitors that the cages were secure. The walls were lined six feet up with steel plates, the doors 'are marvels of strength' – four inch oak with steel plates and beams. '[N]othing less powerful than a locomotive', asserted Hornaday, 'could break through or break down the front bars and beams'. Elephant House resident Victoria, however, gave it her best try. The rhinoceros had a habit of rubbing her horn on the iron bars, so an extra interior pipe fence of galvanized iron was erected in 1915. After being cooped up inside for two weeks straight because of the cold, Victoria was released to the outside area where she immediately charged the fence, bending the two-inch pipe and breaking the upper rail. 'From an examination of this clean break it would appear that a power nothing short of dynamite could effect the damage caused by the charging body of this animal', wrote curator Raymond Ditmars. Interestingly, Ditmars does not attribute this behaviour to the ferocity of an animal trying to escape, suggesting rather that she 'was seized with a desire to play'.[29]

Hornaday too expressed the rhinoceros's desire to play:

> *The Rhinoceros* is a sanguine animal, of rather dull vision and slow understanding. In captivity it gives little trouble, and lives long. Adults individually often become pettish, or peevish, and threaten to prod their keepers without cause, but I have never known a keeper to take those lapses seriously. The average rhino is by no means a dull or a stupid animal, and they have quite enough life to make themselves interesting to visitors.[30]

By the mid-twentieth century the rhinoceros seemed to gain some understanding among those who exhibited and came to view it. It was no longer the dumbest of animals, as Bronx Zoo keeper Dick Richards related in 1944, speaking of the animals in his charge at the Elephant House: 'There is a tapir, too, that has no name at all, for tapirs are stupid animals, hardly worthy, it seems to me, of having names.' Not only did the zoo give its rhinos names, it celebrated them in architecture. And they possessed one rhinoceros that would be immortalized in art.[31]

Bessie was procured by the Bronx Zoo in 1923 from famed animal collector Frank Buck. In the park's annual report, Hornaday wrote she was '[t]he most important addition among the mammals during this past year'. With great difficulty, Buck took the Indian rhinoceros from Nepal. He wired Hornaday on 30 May of that year from Calcutta in code, translated: 'have secured very great cost great trouble rhinos shipping today'. Clearly procuring a rhinoceros was no easy task, but not because it was difficult to capture. The coded message implies a level of secrecy in exporting the animal. It seems, however, that the rhino was worth the trouble.[32]

Weems working on her monument to Bessie.

John T. Benson, an agent for the famed Hagenbeck animal collectors, also procured rhinoceroses for the Bronx Zoo. In 1923 he priced female Indian rhinoceroses at $11,000 for each, while he asked only $6,500 for African male rhinos. The value of a female Indian rhinoceros was strikingly different than those from Africa. The one-horned animal, like the unicorn, was still difficult to obtain. Hornaday knew well the pricing differentials when he wrote to Buck that '[a] rhinoceros from Penang is liable to be either the lesser Indian or the Sumatran, and the difference makes a world of difference in the price and sale', implying that because of the Sumatran's smaller size and lack of attractiveness, it should come at a lesser price.[33]

Buck's rhinoceros, Bessie, was a rare specimen, inspiring a sculpture that stands outside her former home to this day. Katherine Ward Lane Weems used Bessie as a model for her two sculptures, unveiled outside Harvard University's Biological Laboratories Building in 1937, after five years of meticulous work. Named Victoria and Elizabeth (Bessie), after English queens – and former Bronx Zoo rhinos – these respectable names did not prevent the crude pranks of college students. When the curtain was pulled off the sculptures, reported one spectator, bedpans had been placed beneath each rhino.

When Weems was commissioned to choose an unusual animal for the entrance to the Biological Laboratories, she toyed with other ideas, but finally settled on the Indian rhinoceros. She explained her decision:

It occurred to me that here was an animal so prehistoric looking and strange that it certainly would be different . . . while the Black African variety had a more handsome head and horn, the Indian 'Unicornis' had him lashed to the mast when it came to size and armour-plated hide.

Its rarity and interesting texture drew Weems to this specific species. She strove to make her sculpture both accurate and artistic. In addition, she desired to portray them 'in an attitude of suspicion, about to charge'.[34]

Even in her old age, Bessie caught the eye of zoo artists. In 1956 photographer Sam Dunton was told to take a 'dynamic springtime cover shot' of the 'vigorous black rhinoceros', Young Joe. When this rhino came to the zoo a year earlier, Dunton had called him a 'timid rhinoceros', though he explained, that 'is virtually a contradiction in terms'. Startled by noises and even the voices of the keepers, he hid inside for nearly a week, but soon became so accustomed to his surroundings 'that he has learned to beg for popcorn over the stone wall'. The zoo advertised the arrival of Little Joe: 'And another not-likely-to-be-so-endearing baby . . . will take the place of truculent Joe, the Tough Guy of the Elephant House.'[35]

Dunton set his shutter speed too low for the antics of Joe and was about to change it when, from the next cage, the elder Bessie curiously wandered toward him. 'Despite her girth and age, she approached at what was, for her, a brisk trot', remembered Dunton. The shot shows the Indian rhino gesturing towards the camera, with one foot raised in forward motion. It made the cover of the zoo's magazine, *Animal Kingdom*, despite the shots of Young Joe that Dunton did print as assigned.[36]

'A CLOWN PRETENDING TO BE A VERY FIERCE RHINO': CORA

As a boy Hugh Stanton was employed by Theodore Roosevelt to capture small animals in the forests and savannahs of Africa. Hugh was so ambitious and dedicated that Roosevelt had to pay him just to get him to stop bringing new specimens. Raised in Africa, Hugh trained as a white hunter, but his passion for wildlife quickly turned to compassion, as he set about inventing ways to humanely capture rhinoceroses for zoos. Seeing the practice of killing a mother to take her calf as unsuitable, Hugh tested all manner of contraptions. As his partner and wife Jane recalled:

> Hugh designed traps set in the earth, traps that came down from the sky, and all manner of triggered traps. He considered a bag to slip over the animal's head with a pouch of chloroform which would burst, or an outsized hypodermic needle filled with a sleep-inducing drug which could be poised to spear the rhino as he passed by.

Although these contraptions ensnared buffalo, eland and even elephant, the rhinos simply turned the other way. 'We began to appreciate the intelligence that lies in the enormous thick heads of these two-ton beasts', remembered Jane, 'and to wonder if we had any chance of tricking them.'

Rhinoceroses, however, could not resist the call of their taste buds. By winding black No. 10 cotton thread around one of the species' favourite treats – a succulent creeper – the Stantons finally lured their first rhino into a trap. Their task now was to make it behave. The couple became so adept at habituating rhinos to captivity that their catches were sent to zoos around the world. 'The rhino soon learned that a traveling crate was a dining room', wrote Jane. The couple would get the animals used to travelling by truck, and expose them to sounds: 'creaky wheelbarrows, lowing cattle, distant trains, radio music'.

Their first capture, Kamata, was sent to a zoo in South America, where he was known to make 'little pitiful noises' to earn the carrots or sugar lumps the visitors held near his cage.

Another captive, Sally, was sent to the San Diego Zoo and often arranged pebbles in rows. Their most famous rhino, however, did not leave their Kenyan home, known as Bushwhackers. Cora was 'a clown pretending to be a very fierce rhino'. The Stantons indulged her penchant for charging tea tables and attracted the attention of a film crew who gave the rhino a camp-wrecking scene in the film *Mogambo* (1953).[37]

At today's new zoos, rhinoceroses are exhibited and studied. 'Paroxysms of rage' are warded off with enrichment activities – balls filled with treats are attached to rods and the rhinoceros spins the ball to get the treats to fall out. In addition to a regular diet they are given browse (akin to the sweet treats). And their violent reputation seems to have been quashed. On Disney's Animal Kingdom safari ride, rhinos tamely roam in close proximity to vehicles containing tourists, as the narrator tells a conservation narrative about poachers. One Disney rhino, Tex, came with his keeper from the San Antonio Zoo. Breaking with

The Stantons used this photograph of Cora at their sanctuary, Bushwhackers, as their Christmas card one year.

the idea that the rhinoceros is too violent, too stupid or too ugly to form a relationship with humans, then director of the Disney zoo Rick Bolongi described how she rubbed its belly like a puppy and claimed, 'If a rhino could fall in love with a person, Tex would be in love with his keeper . . . '.[38]

A rhino capable of love? What a long road rhinos have travelled. From the formidable enemy of the elephant to Cora the clown, the rhinoceroses put on display in menageries, zoos, and circuses performed important cultural work for their species. Through time and exposure, representations of captive rhinos became ever tamer. But those who encountered rhinos in the wild often told of a very different beast.

3 Native Haunts

The rhino looked so huge, so ridiculous, and so fine to see,
and I sighted on her chest.
Ernest Hemingway (1935)[1]

Beginning in the nineteenth century, the rhinoceros lured
western hunters to Africa, and a few to Asia. Along with other
large game, the rhinoceros became a rare but sought after
trophy of the hunt. Like earlier explorers who sought proof
of the animal's existence, sport hunters desired physical evidence of their animal encounter. The head, the horn, or even the
entire body, represented not the animal's existence, but the skill
of the hunter.

In his hunting tale *Green Hills of Africa* (1935), Ernest
Hemingway revealed complex reactions to rhinoceros hunting.
While the rhino was sublime in its sheer size, its unlikely appearance touched on the absurd. Size preoccupied Hemingway and
many other hunters, who sought to best their hunting buddies
by procuring the largest animal. While tracking and the moment
of encounter are key elements of the experience, the object one
took home was just as important – if not more – than the accompanying tale of the hunt.

In addition to its form, the rhino's ridiculous sublimity was
inspired by its behaviour in the wild. 'Bewilderment' is how
hunter-biologist Herbert Lang characterized its reaction to
human presence. So strong, yet unable to defend itself against
human weaponry, the rhinoceros of hunting expeditions was
a tragic hero. Tales about rhinoceros hunting inevitably

63

Hunting rhino.

A charging rhino.

included two key characteristics of the species that made it a worthy opponent for the hunter: its 'charge' and its elusiveness. To successfully fell a rhinoceros, a hunter had to be both a good tracker and quick in the direct eye of danger. This chapter explores the way hunting tales represented rhinoceros encounters, and the trophies of the hunt, which were brought home as symbols of those encounters.[2]

With brute force, but no knowledge of where to direct its power, the rhinoceros seemed to Hemingway and Lang a relic of the past need for raw strength over the tricks of technology – a trait they admired even as they destroyed it. Coupled with their belief in its inevitable extinction, the sport hunter felt pride in winning a representative of this former relationship between human and nature in which the latter was dominant. As the ridiculous sublime, the rhinoceros represented nostalgia for the dissipating power of nature in the modern age.

William Temple Hornaday devoted a small section of his 1922 text *The Minds and Manners of Wild Animals: A Book of Personal Observations* to 'The Alleged 'Charge' of the Rhinoceros'. 'For half a century African hunters wrote of the assaults of African rhinoceroses on caravans and hunting parties', he explained. 'Those accounts actually established for that animal a reputation for pugnacity.'[3]

In *Illustrations of the Zoology of South Africa*, the superintendent of the South African Museum related the rhino's supposed vicious 'charge' in 1838:

> Its disposition is extremely fierce, and it universally attacks man if it sees him. The usual method of escape adopted by the natives is to climb up a dense high tree, so as to avoid, if possible, being seen. If the animal misses his sight of the fugitive, he immediately gallops off to his haunt; from when it may be inferred that [h]e is not endowed with the power of a keen scent. Should he, however, espy his object in the tree, woe to the unfortunate native: he begins to butt with his horn, strikes and penetrates the tree, and continues piercing it till it falls when his victim seldom escapes being gored to death . . . Having killed his victim, he leaves him without devouring the carcass.[4]

Like the representations of rhinoceros ferocity discussed earlier, the 'charge' of the rhino is one motif of its reaction to human presence in its native haunts. Like the unicorn, the violence is seemingly without reason; like the caged 'paroxysms of rage', the fit goes unexplained.

The mythological behavior of the unicorn is confirmed by this representation of rhinoceroses which portrayed them as not only wild, but violent for the sake of violence itself. While not a carnivore, they will apparently always attack humans without provocation. The native tradition of escape by tree is described as a game of survival; the fact that the rhino does not eat the carcass makes the death a sacrifice to wildness itself. This is not survival of the fittest, where one animal dies so another may live by consuming him. Instead the human death serves only to prove the animal's ferocity.

When famed British hunter and adventure writer R. Gordon Cumming sighted a bull 'borele', a native term for black rhinoceros, within a hundred yards, he fired. The injury was not enough to fell the rhino, and it turned towards the hunter. '[T]he villain charged', remembered Cumming, 'blowing loudly, and chased me around the bush. Had his activity been equal to his ugliness, my wanderings would have terminated here, but

R. Gordon Cumming on the run.

by my superior agility I had the advantage in the turn.' The rhino then turned away, huffing and 'erecting his insignificant yet saucy-looking tail'. As he did so, he left Cumming 'master of the field', as the hunter shot through the rhino's ribs 'to teach him manners'.[5]

Cumming's prideful telling of the borele reveals a hunter's ego, but suggests an affinity of the human with the rhinoceros – a challenge not between man and beast, but between two potential 'masters' of the field. The black rhino was his villain throughout, and he distinguished the behaviour of different species, as well as assigning them names used by natives: two-horned black: 'keitloa', common white: 'muchocho' and long-horned white: 'kobaoba'. From his encounters, Cumming generalized rhinoceros behaviour, writing that black rhinoceroses were 'extremely fierce and dangerous, and rush, headlong and unprovoked at any object which attracts their attention'. He also agreed with the assessment that black rhinos were 'subject

Death fall of a rhino, captured on film by Martin Johnson.

to paroxysms of unprovoked fury' in which they ploughed up the ground and attacked bushes. This uncontrolled fury aroused biblical allusions for Cumming as he quoted Job: 'Canst thou bind the unicorn with this band in the furrow? Or will he harrow the valleys after thee?'[6]

Holding on to the association of the rhinoceros with native tales and biblical descriptions, Cumming *expected* the charging ferocity of the rhinoceros. Despite his ability to avoid any fatal encounters with the animal, he portrayed another as a 'hideous monster' whose 'horn was completely worn down with age and the violence of his disposition'. '[H]e followed me at such a furious pace for several hundred yards with his horrid horny snout within a few yards of my horse's tail.' Again, the rhinoceros left Cumming alone as soon as he was out of its way, but Cumming insisted on reinforcing his preconceptions of rhino behaviour and intentions.[7]

Initially, president and adventurer Theodore Roosevelt's accounts of rhinoceros behavior in *African Game Trails* (1910) followed a similar vein. At the beginning of his 1910 expedition to Africa, he listed the rhinoceros among the 'dangerous game of Africa' accompanied by the lion, buffalo, elephant and leopard. Roosevelt's fears were due in part to tales he had heard of other injurious hunts which portrayed the fatal charge of the rhinoceros as natural behaviour. A 1907 surveyor, he wrote, was charged 'without provocation', and another hunter was rumoured to be 'deliberately . . . hunted down' and thrown by a rhino for no reason at all.

Roosevelt acknowledged the diversity of animal encounters, where not only the animal's character but circumstance contributes to the danger of an animal. After landing a good shot on the rhino, Roosevelt explained that while a lion would have fallen immediately from the wound, 'the vitality of the huge

Osa Johnson and Vern Karstens celebrating her rhino kill.

pachyderm was so great, its mere bulk counted for so much, that even such a hard-hitting rifle as my double-Holland . . . could not stop it outright.' Roosevelt's hunt was more than one man against a rhinoceros, it was a test of technology over nature.

In addition to its resistance to weaponry, the rhinoceros' sudden charge threatened Roosevelt and his party more than once. As they approached a rhino unaware of the creeping party, '[s]o little did he dream of our presence that when we were a hundred yards off he actually lay down'. When Roosevelt stepped from his protective bush, the rhino immediately 'jumped to his feet with the agility of a polo pony'. No longer peaceful and oblivious, the 'great bull rhino' headed toward them in a determined and 'wicked charge', intent on 'mischief' and '[p]loughing up the ground with horn and feet'. It took three shots to fell the rhino. The right barrel of Roosevelt's double Holland pierced its lungs and it began to charge in the direction of the shot. The left barrel entered its heart, and the final blow came from his companion, ripping into the animal's neck.

Roosevelt's next rhino, however, surprised him. While tracking hippo 'there was a succession of snorts in our front and the sound of the trampling of heavy feet and of a big body being shoved through a dense mass of tropical bush'. This amorphous mass quickly defined itself as a rhinoceros, tossing its head around, showing 'every symptom of being bent on mischief'. Although Roosevelt said he did not consider this rhino a great prize because of the smallness of its horns, the already charging animal left him no choice but to shoot. In three shots, the rhino went silent, but was lost in the dense brush of the riverside. As the party cautiously looked for the animal, Roosevelt recognized that, unlike the earlier hunt where men had the advantage of better eyesight, here the rhino was the one with the sensory advantage: 'The thicket was a tangle of thorn-bushes, reed, and small, low-branching trees; it was impossible to see ten feet through it, and a man could only penetrate it with the utmost slowness and difficulty, whereas the movements of the rhino were very little impeded.'

With some regret, Roosevelt killed a small female rhino that came running towards him as he approached this dead bull. 'Now I did not want to kill this rhinoceros', wrote Roosevelt, 'and I am not certain that it really intended to charge us.' Admitting some lack of knowledge of animal behaviour contributed to his jumping the gun, Roosevelt defended his actions. 'Often under such circumstances the rhino does not mean to charge at all', he explained, 'and is acting in a spirit of truculent and dull curiosity; but often when its motions and actions are indistinguishable from those of an animal that does not mean mischief, it turns out that a given rhino does mean mischief.'

Rather than contributing to all rhinoceroses a penchant for deadly charges, Roosevelt recognized various intentions of the animals, and the human's inability to interpret those intentions in the moment of encounter.

[A]gain and again hunters who do not wish to kill rhinos have been forced to do so in order to prevent mischief. Under such circumstances it is not to be expected that men will take too many chances when face to face with a creature whose actions are threatening and whose intentions it is absolutely impossible to divine.

The problem, continued Roosevelt, is more than a threat to human life in the fleeting moment of the charge. 'I do not see', he lamented, 'how the rhinoceros can be permanently preserved, save in very out-of-the-way places or in regular game reserves' as 'the beast's stupidity, curiosity, and truculence make up a combination of qualities which inevitably tend to insure its destruction.' Valuing the rhinoceros as worth saving, but acknowledging the problems inherent in doing so, Roosevelt called the rhinoceros stupid. This stupidity referred to the rhino's lack of knowledge about the intentions of hunters. Although Roosevelt claimed hunters had a similar lack of familiarity with rhino intentions, it is the animal that is left with the blame.[8]

Following Roosevelt, hunters of the early twentieth century continued to call the rhinoceros's charge into question. Hornaday explained that the supposed 'evil intentions of the rhinoceros' are 'nothing more nor less than a movement to draw nearer to the strange man-object, on account of naturally poor vision, to see what men look like'. Similarly, Lang described his sense of rhino 'bewilderment' as 'hesitation and fear, [which] may be the natural result of their inability to define clearly what danger confronts them'. Recognition of the rhino's poor eyesight transformed its reputation from ferocious to curious, and its intentions from strange to familiar. 'In reality', explained Hornaday, like the humans gazing upon it, when the rhinoceros charges 'it is only desiring a "close-up" to satisfy its legitimate curiosity'.[9]

Game was so plentiful on Roosevelt's safari that as soon as he felled an eland, a 'Wakamba' man ran to him to report a rhinoceros sighting on a nearby hillside. Along with Slatter, the guide and a gun-bearer, Roosevelt easily approached the rhino as they were upwind of the creature. They hid behind a bush which they could see through but the poor vision of the rhino's 'small, piglike eyes' could not. 'The big beast stood like an uncouth statue', wrote Roosevelt, 'his hide black in the sunlight; he seemed what he was, a monster surviving over from the world's past, from the days when the beasts of the prime ran riot in their strength, before man grew so cunning of brain and hand as to master them.' Just as the prehistoric image of the rhinoceros represented a counterpoint to civilization, felling a rhino was a symbol of a man's daring.

Like Cumming, Roosevelt called the rhinoceros a 'monster'. Despite its familiar eyes, the rhinoceros is ultimately strange, a relic of the prehistoric, and a symbol of massive strength. It reminded Roosevelt of a day when sheer power was the rule of survival, instead of the cleverness of modern man and his technologies. The rhinoceros represented the power of nature in an era when, as Roosevelt would argue, men were being effeminized by modern work and conditions.

Still, it was the inventions of the modern era that enabled Roosevelt to kill the rhino. In doing so, Roosevelt used the body of the rhinoceros to learn about the power of his two different guns – the Winchester and the Holland – making the body of the rhinoceros a testing ground for technological efficiency. The Winchester's bullets did mortal damage, but the Holland's instilled a 'smashing blow', penetrating even the rhino's heavy bones. A later encounter challenged Roosevelt to use his

Springfield, but after eight bullets and a six-and-a-half kilometre chase, he proclaimed the Holland the winner.[10]

In both the elusiveness and the charging threat of the rhinoceros, hunters found an animal trophy to represent their quickness of mind and gun. But not just any rhino would do. Roosevelt's ideal rhinoceros had 'a big body and good horn'. A true trophy need be large to be impressive.

Hemingway agreed. In *Green Hills of Africa* the narrator, standing in for Hemingway himself, shoots one and is immediately impressed with his catch, exclaiming, '[t]his was the hell of an animal'. Meanwhile, his rival Karl has downed another rhino – one double the size of his. Unable to truly feel anything other

Lydekker's African rhinoceros.

than jealousy upon seeing his rival's 'dream rhino', 'whose small-er horn was longer than our big one', another man in the party tries to console the narrator by complimenting his excellent shot. 'The hell with that shot', he replies with irritation, 'That bloody fluke. God, what a beautiful rhino.'

It is not the hunting skill here that boosts the hunter's ego, but the size of his kill. Frustrated, he calls his prize 'a lousy runt', and laments that Karl's 'makes mine ridiculous'. Though Hemingway makes clear that Karl is not the better hunter and a lousy shot, he was walking away from Africa with tangible results – and that is apparently what mattered most. The situa-tion is too much for him to bear, as he rants:

> he had beaten me. Not only beaten, beaten was all right. He had made my rhino look so small that I could never keep him in the same small town where we lived. He had wiped him out. I had the shot I had made on him to remember and nothing could take that away except that it was so bloody marvelous I knew I would wonder, sooner or later, if it was not really a fluke in spite of my unholy self-confidence. Old Karl had put it on us all right with that rhino.[11]

Souvenir size was key to proving the prowess of the hunter. And physical proof of an encounter with an enormous animal was necessary for, as Pop points out when another party reported seeing a huge rhino: 'Of course nearly any rhino would look huge when he was chasing him.' With one last lament, the nar-rator reflects, 'I don't give a damn about these rhino outside of the fun of hunting them. But I'd like to get one that wouldn't look silly beside that dream rhino of his.' His hunting goal has become the competition of procuring the best rhinoceros, not the fun of the hunt or the thrill of animal encounter. The rhinoceros trophy is a symbol of his own self-worth, not only as a hunter, but as a man.[12]

'Among living giants', wrote Theodore Roosevelt of the northern white rhinoceros, 'it is the only one that has been considered extinct, the only one never brought alive to civilized countries.' The elusiveness of this subspecies in a densely vegetated landscape, and their mostly nocturnal activities, made study of their lives nearly impossible. Their value was greater dead than alive, and their 'trails and tracks' provided evidence of their habits 'supplied so seldom by face to face encounters'.

After Major Powell-Cotton publicized an area called the Lado District, where white rhinoceros were plenty, Roosevelt and Lang organized separate expeditions to rediscover and collect these rhinos. Even in museum collections, reported Roosevelt, mounted specimens were rare. The hunts of Lang and Roosevelt were symbolic trips back in time; their subsequent trophies symbolically revived an animal from extinction. The elusiveness of the subspecies made such prizes that much more meaningful. Procuring an elusive white rhinoceros was proof of hunting prowess.

Because they fit the bill of a worthy opponent in size, elusiveness, and violence, bagging a white rhinoceros was the sign of a manly hunter, while the subsequent exhibition of the prize invoked national pride. In challenging his contemporaries to capture a white rhinoceros alive, Lang articulated:

Is any American sportsman willing to help capture so coveted a prize? . . . to be the first to exhibit a monster that

A freshly killed white rhinoceros used for the diorama in the Akeley Hall of African Mammals, American Museum of Natural History, New York.

has successfully daunted skill and courage? It would be a fitting and well deserved triumph for one of America's leading institutions, which, backed by keen enterprising spirit, has aroused the admiration and envy of century-old competitors abroad.

The white rhino in the Bronx would stand, expounded Lang, for the superiority of American institutions. 'Shall America be first?,' he concluded his expedition report.

When Lang set out for white rhino territory in 1909 he aimed to collect skins and skulls for museum exhibition, not living specimens. Acting as Assistant Curator of Mammalogy for the American Museum of Natural History and Chairman of the Subcommittee on Life Histories of Exotic Mammals for the American Society of Mammalogists, Lang led his expedition into the Congo. This expedition had to take diplomatic measures to collect their desired rarity. Since Roosevelt had entered the region earlier that year, the Colonial Administration vowed not to let anyone else hunt the small herd of white rhinos in its Uele district. Lang and his partner James P. Chapin told them they planned to join with Roosevelt in their quest for 'a realistic bit of the greatness and fascination of the African jungles'. They were admitted, but Lang's expedition was delayed while trying to procure okapi and never did unite with Roosevelt's party (if that was their intention at all).

Featured prominently on the first page of Lang's expedition report in the *Bulletin of the New York Zoological Society* is a white rhinoceros looking ferocious even in death. The caption tells us this record-breaking bull had a 107-cm front horn that, along with the rear one, 'acts as a fender in thrusting aside obstructions in the jungle'. The horn record was held by Gordon Cumming, at 158 cm; Lang's record was for the two largest whole specimens of rhino bodies, a bull and a cow, which appear to be the ones on display at the American Museum of Natural History.[13]

Meanwhile, Roosevelt's safari returned with an assortment of white rhino specimens. In 1910 he donated a head to the National Collection of Heads and Horns, one of Hornaday's pet projects, housed at the Bronx Zoo. Hornaday praised the head

The National Collection of Heads and Horns, with a rhinoceros head at back left.

The artist who painted the backdrop to AMNH's white rhinoceros diorama, William Leigh, sketched out this specimen in the field.

W. R. LEIGH.

as 'worthy to stand as a gift from the foremost sportsman of the world'. For it was no ordinary hunter who could fell a white rhinoceros, and no ordinary specimen should represent the revered hunter in the 'national' collection.

The National Collection of Heads and Horns was the recipient of gifts from sportsmen around the world – British East Africa, Kashmir, London, Philadelphia, Pittsburgh, Doylestown, Victoria, Santa Barbara and China. The horns broke records for at least sixteen species, including Cape Buffalo and Greater Kudu. Acquisition was secured by procuring grand specimens, if not record breaking. Hornaday wrote that the bison was not represented because 'a thoroughly *satisfactory* head is not easy to find, nor easy to procure when found. A mediocre head will not serve.'[14]

The mounting of Roosevelt's white rhinoceros head, done by James L. Clark, was to Hornaday 'exceedingly perfect and lifelike . . . beyond the reach of adverse criticism'. This 'grand prize' possessed the second largest horn Roosevelt had brought back; his other specimens went to the National Museum in

Washington, DC. With more than a little nationalism associated with this procurement of the 'white' animal of darkest Africa, Hornaday claimed: 'The fact that the National Museum now contains the finest existing collection of specimens of the White Rhinoceros should be a source of pride to the Society.' The importance of the collections was highlighted by biologist Madison Grant. It represented, he proclaimed, 'the inexorable disappearance of the grand game animals of the world and the imperative necessity of gathering now the collections that will adequately represent them hereafter when remnants of the wild species of to-day will exist only in protected game preserves, or not at all.'[15]

Although to our twenty-first-century minds it seems a contradictory practice, hunters believed samples of disappearing wildlife were serving the interest of humanity and nature; they were salvaging specimens before their inevitable disappearance. This Noah's Ark mentality was behind the National Collection of Heads and Horns, as well as many other museum collecting expeditions around the globe. The disappearance of these animals in the wild, especially large game, was thought assured. Hunters saw the development of wildlife preserves as an affront to the wildness of game, and wanted to collect before they were entrapped and 'tamed'. Indeed, it was the elusiveness of game that made them worthy of the hunt.

NEW LIFE FOR DEAD RHINOS

Nearly as elusive, though much more predictable, stuffed rhinoceroses stand silent and waiting in natural history museums around the world. From Louis the XV's eighteenth-century Versailles menagerie rhino, stuffed behind glass at the Muséum National d'Histoire Naturelle in the Jardin des Plantes, Paris, to

Lang's anonymous rhinos in New York, natural history museums combine the arts of hunting, preserving and sculpting animals. The animals on display were carefully rendered and the backgrounds artistically and accurately reproduced. The spoils of the hunt were resurrected for public viewing through the craft of art and the skills of science.

James L. Clark was employed as artist and taxidermist by the American Museum of Natural History. He was also praised for his construction of a group of white rhinos, apparently procured by Roosevelt, at the Carnegie Museum. 'Clark's group of three Rooseveltian white rhinoceroses is a grand piece of work', wrote Hornaday, continuing with an explanation of the challenges of rhinoceros exhibition. Whereas smaller animals were easily posed and arranged in the small space of a display case, similar artistry is 'out of the question in any rhinoceros group installed in a case that really is too small for it'.[16]

Clark's skill in realistically resurrecting rhinos came in part from his travels with field collecting expeditions to observe wild rhinos and their landscapes. Striving for the accuracy of visual representation of the animal and its landscape, Clark explained

Clark kept a sketchbook while on expedition, in which he detailed rhinoceros features, such as the ears.

Black Rhino

Clark's sketches of a Black rhinoceros at rest. Such careful field observations made his taxidermy accurate.

in a radio interview: 'It is absolutely necessary for our staff to have that firsthand information which one can get only by personal contact. So into these groups go the accuracy, color and inspiration which the artist himself saw and felt.'[17]

From the sketchbook he kept while on expedition in Africa, the observations necessary for rhino resurrection are made clear. Clark sketched close examinations of rhino ears, feet, tails. There are views of rhinos from the front, the back, standing, and lying down. These details were then used as visual cues when creating the models for the museum display. As the hunter attempted to understand rhinoceros behavior, the artist carefully observed its posture, movements and physical features.[18]

Combining his observations with the trophies of the hunt, Clark gave new homes to dead rhinos. He described the process of resurrecting specimens from the field. First, the sculptor-taxidermist set the skeleton on a supporting frame, chose a pose, then covered the structure with clay. A mould of cheesecloth, wire and papier mâché was made of the sculpted clay structure. The mould was separated in half, retaining about 4 mm thickness, after which the model was thrown away. The two halves were pieced back together, the tanned skin pasted on the mould and arranged to resemble the observations of the artist in the field. With a glass eye and a bit of paint to render eyes and nose realistic, Clark said, 'the animal lives again'.[19]

Set in exhibit cases, with real tree trunks (though leaves of wax) and actual dirt from the locale, the resurrected animals

Skinning a rhino – the first act of preserving its body.

Using the skeleton to shape the recreation.

Moulding the form.

Nearing completion.

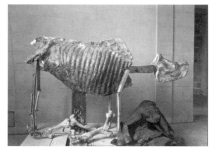

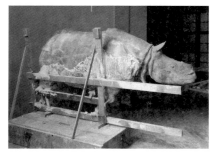

were then illuminated 'until it all becomes as real as if one was looking out of a train window in a far away land'. Clark continued: 'We cannot take you there, but in our way, we can bring bits of this far-off land here, for you to study and enjoy.'[20]

The result of Clark's observations and work is still on display in the American Museum's Akeley Hall of African Mammals. As Clark desired, the visitor today is transported to a 'far-off land' and can 'study and enjoy' the rhinoceroses. But there is an element to viewing these exhibits that is unspoken. The stories of procuring these specific rhinoceroses is just as much an artefact of their presence as the artists behind the exhibit. They are intended to be anonymous objects for scientific and artistic contemplation. But their existence as trophies of the hunt – of specific encounters of named hunters and individual rhinoceroses – is an untold tale that reveals much about how rhinos have been understood.

Although museums leave the rhinos anonymous in their labelling, it is possible to trace their journey from the wild to the museum. The stories behind these exhibits also reveal the value

Model of the diorama.

of rhinos as cultural objects. The discussion of white rhinoceroses continued from the field hunting of Roosevelt and Lang into the public realm, concerned about the survival of the white rhino exhibit at the American Museum of Natural History.

Even in exhibition, the white rhinoceros retain their mystery. While most display cases are labelled with donor names in gilded letters beneath the glass, the white rhinoceros has no such detail. It appears they were collected by the Lang-Chapin Expedition in the Upper Nile River district of Zaire, years before the hall was begun. When it came time to mount the specimens, donors balked, preferring to donate to exhibits for animals not yet collected. Some donors collected the animals themselves, donating the trophies, as well as money to paint, pose and adorn the cases. They seemingly wanted the glory of hunting the specimens themselves.[21]

The Akeley Hall of African Mammals was begun by Carl Akeley, whose untimely death on expedition in Africa inspired the naming of the exhibit space and donations for its completion in his memory. Akeley had apparently begun taxidermy of the white rhino specimens before Clark, but museum president Trubee Davison had difficulty obtaining funds to complete the diorama. He wrote to Akeley's widow that he was pouring funds into the display in hopes of obtaining a later donation to cover its $10,000 cost.[22]

Even the public was aware of the tragedy of the unfunded white rhinoceroses. *New York Herald* published an editorial by H. E. Aisch of Yonkers on 23 February 1937. Aisch wrote: 'It has been the express wish of Mrs. Akeley that a white rhinoceros group which had been well started by Mr. Akeley should be finished. Might I ask that some public spirited person suggest some means of raising the funds so that this great, lasting educational exhibit may more nearly approach its completion?' One month

later came a hopeful, but inconclusive reply stating the New York City Board of Education 'would be glad of the opportunity to complete one or more of these unfinished exhibits'. When the hall opened in 1941, the white rhinos, along with colobus monkey and leopard, were still unfinanced, though complete.[23]

Gazing upon the white rhinoceros case at the American Museum of Natural History, one is not told the back story, and is in fact encouraged to forget that it exists. The rhino's individuality, the hunting prowess of Herbert Lang, the careful observations of Clark and the competition to procure a rare species for a prestigious American institution, are ignored in favour of more generalized information about rhinoceroses. The label tells of the region from which it came and explains general facts about rhino habits and habitat.

The complete white rhinoceros diorama in the Akeley Hall of African Mammals, AMNH.

Rather than deny the hunt implicit in creating the exhibit, museums could recognize the individuality of encounter. Instead of pretending to know all rhinos from the specimens on view, we could lay claim to a very specific human encounter with specific rhinoceroses. As Roosevelt insisted, we may not know what all rhinos will do in any given circumstance. By telling the stories behind their specimens, museums have the opportunity to breathe life and drama into their exhibits.

COLLECTING GLIMPSES

Their elusiveness in the early twentieth century led to the desire to collect and resurrect rhinoceroses, but on Redmond O'Hanlon's journey, near the end of the century, he sought only a glimpse of the elusive rhinoceros of Borneo. Seeking the satisfaction of knowing the animal exists in the wild implies a different concept of animal encounter than was previously sought. Hunting encounters, by definition, required trophies. O'Hanlon's exploration chased only the visual.

Today the most elusive of the species is the Sumatran rhinoceros. In *Into the Heart of Borneo* (1984), British adventure-writer O'Hanlon wrote of setting his sights on these island jungles, where he hoped to 're-discover the Borneo rhinoceros'. When he informed a government officer of his goal, the man replied, 'I am afraid that that is impossible.' Explaining that the territory they inhabit is unmapped, dangerous and too remote for officials to go if the party needed rescuing, he firmly stated the journey was '[o]ut of the question'. Fortunately for O'Hanlon, a letter from Oxford University persuaded the government to let him proceed.

Travelling up the Rajang and Baleh Rivers in Sarawak, O'Hanlon questioned native communities about the rhinoceros.

The native Kenyah had all heard of its existence but never sighted one. Some hundred years earlier, Charles Hose looked for rhino in Borneo, calling the species 'quite the most grotesque of his kind'. Like Hose, O'Hanlon found salt licks, mud baths and trampled vegetation, and his heart skipped with the thought of a nearby rhino. But the would-be moment of re-discovery became a comedy as his guides began to laugh and snort, indicating these were 'babi' or pig tracks.

As O'Hanlon continued his journey through a world of a seemingly endless amount of leeches, he encountered more birds than mammals, more people than rhinoceros. He headed to the villages of the Ukit, 'the men who could tell us, if anyone could, whether or no the Borneo rhinoceros was still to be found'. In their community, only one had ever seen the rhinoceros – an old man who sat quietly away from the scorn of the younger generation. They said he was old and stupid, but in his youth was a legendary hunter who 'ran so fast he could catch the birds in their flight'. O'Hanlon approached the old Ukit and showed him pictures of birds and mammals from field guides. The man smiled with recognition at the illustrations. When O'Hanlon flipped to the page displaying a photograph of a rhinoceros, the man was filled with 'wild intensity'. He told of spearing eight such animals in his youth. 'Our search', O'Hanlon concluded his book, 'has ended'.[24]

It is an odd ending to an expedition. There was no triumphal return to civilization, no discovery of the animal he sought, no trophies to mount. O'Hanlon's search ends not with the rhinoceros, but with one man's intimate knowledge of the animal. The search, it seems, was not for an animal, but for a certain kind of heroics, for a certain type of manhood of which the rhinoceros is symbolic, and perhaps for an experience of an idealized human–animal relationship. O'Hanlon's intended rediscovery

had little nobility to it. What good would his sighting a rhinoceros in Borneo have done? He admitted, if it was akin to discovery at all, that it was 're-discovery'. The nobler revelation, implied O'Hanlon, is that a man still existed who knew the Sumatran rhinoceros as something other than an elusive ghost or mounted trophy.

If this man is what O'Hanlon had been looking for all along, if meeting him stands for an encounter with an actual rhinoceros, then what are we to think of the rhinoceros? Although O'Hanlon's transferral of discovery onto the native is indicative of western sentimentality towards native peoples, the old Ukit man represents a relationship with rhinoceroses which is close to passing. As the rhinoceros is endangered, so is the human experience with it as a wild animal. As their habitat disappears, and they are taken from the wild for protection, the Sumatran rhinoceros is losing its 'wildness'. In a way, this man may be the last human who knows what it is to see a wild Sumatran rhinoceros.

4 Cultural Life

Tin Man: 'Would you be afraid of a rhinoceros?'
Lion: 'Imposserous.'
The Wizard of Oz (1939)

Every story must have its enemy – the one who stirs up trouble, endangers lives and inspires dread in the audience. For how can we have heroes and heroines without villains? For exploring film-makers Martin and Osa Johnson, the rhinoceros was 'public enemy number one'. Shooting films on the African plains during the first decades of the twentieth century, the Johnsons made some of the first documentary recordings of the continent's wildlife. Although their footage and lectures were presented in educational settings and used by museums, to keep money flowing for production, the husband and wife duo released popular feature films which dramatized their animal encounters.

Born and bred in Kansas, before journeying to Africa Martin and Osa knew rhinos only from their cultural image. It appears they had not even seen one in captivity. The encounter in *Congorilla* (1932) is typical of their creation of the filmic wild rhinoceros. Osa yelled at it, shot her gun to scare it, and approached it in an attempt to get it to come closer to the camera. While they insisted on getting such footage, and portraying their encounter with rhinos as spontaneous and dangerous ones, this is not how they themselves experienced rhino encounters. It took much provoking to get the close shots their films reveal. This active intervention to create what they would have called 'authentic'

From the comic strip *Safari Trails*.

Osa Johnson with the rhino she shot with gun and camera.

rhinoceros footage reveals their cultural blinders, that is, their expectations for wildlife behaviour interfered with 'natural' animal behaviour.

The images and assumptions about rhinoceroses discussed thus far reveal attempts to know the real animal. This chapter addresses the ways in which rhinoceroses have been deliberately fictionalized. In endowing rhinos with personalities, authors and artists have exaggerated the traits already observed for centuries.

Martin Johnson lending his hat to 'Public Enemy No. 1'.

Many also creatively imagine the origins of this behaviour. Antagonistic, dim-witted and even beautiful, fictional rhinoceroses portray the species at its best – and its worst.

ANTAGONISTIC

In his real-life encounters Herbert Lang claimed he found more adventure in photographing animals than in shooting them. While attempting to get a picture, a rhino charged leaving Lang running for a clump of trees. When he stopped, the rhino was directly behind. Fortunately, the trees were in a tight enough clump that the rhino could not get through, ensuring Lang's safety.

Afterwards, Lang's companion, who had witnessed the scene, asked why he had fumbled for his right pocket when so cornered by the rhino. 'I wanted my spare glasses', Lang replied, 'not to lose one precious moment of a spectacle one cannot see twice'. Conflating animal amusements with real encounters,

Petroglyphs from
Twyfeltontein,
Namibia.

Lang related his experience to a Hollywood creation. '[I]t had all the settings of a movie story', claimed Lang, somewhat regretfully adding, 'and with not even a line of pictures to show.'[1]

The Johnsons sought such footage, and did experience close calls with wildlife, including rhinoceroses. But capturing life-threatening encounters as they occurred was near impossible. Thus upon meeting an uninterested rhinoceros they would do all they could to provoke an exciting encounter. They sought authenticity and new knowledge of animals, but they also sought an audience hungry for action and adventure. Although possibly as elusive in western culture as in the wild, imagined rhinoceroses are often even more pointlessly violent than the portrayal of their living counterparts. For many, as for the Johnsons, the rhinoceros is 'Public Enemy Number One'.

Real safari expeditions inspired a whole genre of Hollywood films. As for Martin and Osa Johnson, experience and cultural representation were greatly tangled in perceptions of rhinoceroses. Transplanted cowboy John Wayne rounds up African animals in the 1962 film *Hatari*. The film begins with a rhino chase by jeep, in which the animal furiously attacks the car and stabs a veteran animal trapper in the leg. We soon learn that the young woman at the centre of a love quadrangle had been left alone in Africa when a rhinoceros killed her father. Though the encounter is never described, this, along with the first rhino attack scene, leaves the animal looming in the background as the ultimate danger of the African plains. The injured man even requests the others not to go after rhino this season, as there must be a curse. Despite the supposed curse, the last animal-trapping scene is with a rhinoceros. Again, the animal continually charges up to the jeep, but this time they capture the raging rhino, putting a definite end to its wild behaviour.

While John Wayne was more often taming the wilds of the American frontier, in *Hatari* the rhinoceros is chosen as the ultimate wild beast for him to confront in the African bush. Another pairing of rhinoceros with manly movie hero pits Indiana Jones against the creature. In *Indiana Jones and the Last Crusade* (1989) the young Indiana runs from bad guys aboard a train and leaps onto the roof of the cars carrying circus animals. As he jumps onto one which seems safe, a rhinoceros, apparently startled by the noise, pierces through the ceiling with its horn, protruding right between Indiana's parted legs – threatening a very important region of the adventure hero's masculinity.

Fictional rhinos do not only attack iconic male heroes, however. Sometimes they have no provocation for their attacks. In *James and the Giant Peach* (1961) British children's author Roald Dahl casts a belligerent rhino in the despicable role of orphaning a young boy. In a story in which a four-year-old boy befriends a variety of talking and singing insects, the action is spurred by an anonymous rhinoceros who, having escaped from London Zoo, ate James's parents 'in full daylight, mind you, and on a crowded street . . . in thirty-five seconds flat'.

While these accounts do not explain the violence of rhinoceroses, other cultural representations do make the attempt. An East African tale places the blame with one forgetful rhinoceros and one greedy giraffe. 'How Giraffe Got Such a Long Neck . . . and Why Rhino is So Grumpy' tells of a time of drought on the plains which left all the animals scrambling for what little vegetation remained on the ground. Frustrated at the plentitude of green leaves growing at the tops of acacia trees, Giraffe turned to Rhinoceros who, equally upset at not being able to reach this tempting food, replied in his gruff manner, 'oomphhh'. Since neither animal was equipped to climb trees, Rhinoceros suggests seeing the human witchdoctor. When they reach his home the healer agrees to give them a 'magic herb' which will make their necks grow long enough to reach the treetops. He tells them to return in the morning, but only Giraffe remembers. Having found some fresh grass, the absent-minded Rhinoceros forgets. When he arrives, it is too late – the witchdoctor had given all the herb to Giraffe who had grown a long, elegant neck enabling him to reach all the food atop the acacia trees. Jealous and upset, when Rhinoceros sees the witchdoctor, he angrily charges in his direction. All rhinoceroses, the tale teaches, hold a grudge against humans and, when seeing them are reminded of this witchdoctor, and charge in a resentful fit.[2]

Cultural rhinos have been known to hold their ground against humans for reasons other than their own forgetfulness. Since 1955 a single rhinoceros has been holding a group of men up a palm tree, threatening them with his horn, in a scene reminiscent of nineteenth-century natural history descriptions, supposedly drawn from the experiences of native Africans. His eye is ferocious, his head moves up and down, nearly prodding the bottom man's bum. This rhinoceros is not made of flesh and blood, but stuffed with the 'magic' of Disney.

When Disneyland opened in California, one of the inaugural rides was the Jungle Cruise. This boat ride through the tropical forests of three continents is different from most other Disney rides in two ways: one, the animals do not talk and two, live actors guide the visitors' experiences and the narration of the ride. These tour guides distil the danger and humour of the Jungle landscape. Passing the rhino-treed men, they quip: 'That rhino seems to be getting his point across, and I'm sure that guy on the bottom will get it in the end!'

The men up the tree mock facial expressions of fear, but they are cartoon-like, exaggerated. The animatronic rhinoceros thrusts its horn upwards in a stand-off without end, turning a

As visitors pass this scene, Jungle Cruise guides quip, 'I think they'll get the point in the end.'

life-threatening situation into a comic encounter. On the other hand, the rhino has won the battle for the moment. Although the rhinoceros is violent, he is not pointlessly so. The men up the tree are poachers, not innocent tourists like those on the boat. The Jungle Cruise rhino then is a moral being. Scary . . . but just.

When rhinoceroses are not directing their anger towards humans, fictional accounts fall back on the long heritage of elephant–rhinoceros enmity. In the book that introduced audiences to Babar the Elephant, French writer-illustrator Jean de Brunhoff casts rhinoceroses as violent, but it is their feud with elephants that lies behind their behaviour. However, a few rhinos appear in marginal roles in which they peacefully attend the wedding of the elephant king and queen, Babar and Celeste, just crowned because of Babar's knowledge of human ways. In one of the oddest imaginings of a rhinoceros, Brunhoff draws one dancing at the reception with a hippopotamus. In the sequel, *The Travels of Babar* (1934), however, rhinos appear as nothing but bad-tempered antagonists.

While Babar and Celeste embark on an ill-fated honeymoon in a hot air balloon, Babar's young cousin, Arthur, finds mischief at home by tying a firecracker to the tail of sleeping Rataxes the rhinoceros. His pride wounded by the prank,

Babar's nemesis, Rataxes.

Rataxes seeks revenge. When Babar returns home, he finds his elephant subjects at war with the rhinoceroses, who easily overpower them.

At the rhinoceros camp, Rataxes talks with General Pamir about the imminent defeat of the elephants. They are both wearing helmets and breastplates attached to each other by heavy link chains. Even the armoured rhinoceros, it seems, needs more armour for warfare. But Babar's superior intelligence wards off the dim witted rhino army. Fearful that their strength could not overcome that of the rhinos, the elephants paint huge eyes on their bottoms, colour their tails red to look like giant noses, and attach green and red wigs. When the rhinos see the elephants' disguised rear ends, they run in fright, mistaking them for monsters. Pamir and Rataxes are caged and 'hang their heads in shame'.[3]

While rhinos begin as violent and vengeful, they end shamed for their stupidity. This is one of the only successful attempts to make rhinoceroses comical. Brunhoff's illustrations render the rhinos cute, through beady eyes and the thin line of their slightly upturned mouths. They seem to be smiling, even when plotting their vengeful war. Even as Brunhoff plays off typical motifs of elephant–rhino rivalry and its antagonistic personality, the end result of this behaviour is thwarted by their inferior intelligence.

RIDICULOUS

Stupidity is a double-edged personality flaw for the rhinoceros. While it is often viewed as the reason for violence, it also often undermines such ferocious portrayals. African tales discuss the elephant–rhinoceros rivalry and the dangers of the rhino's ignorant pride. One day Elephant is teasing Rhino about his temper and bad eyesight when Rhino challenges him to a contest to see who could make the largest pile of poo. Upon losing the ridiculous challenge, Elephant grew so angry he attacked Rhino, who begged him to stop, and left him within an inch of his life. Properly instilled with fear at challenging the elephant's superiority, rhinoceroses now scatter their dung so that that of elephants will always appear larger.[4]

The Ndebele also believe in elephant–rhino rivalry, and in the elephant's superior strength, but portray the rhino as a sadly stupid character, not one whose ignorance causes violence. Badly wounded by Elephant, Rhino seeks Porcupine hoping to borrow a quill to sew up his wounds. Although the nocturnal animal was unhappy about being awakened, she lent Rhino her best quill with his promise to return it when finished. Sewing his wounds with baobab tree fibre, Rhino created the rough ridges on his skin seen to this day. Exhausted, he fell asleep, the quill beside him. When he awoke he forgot about the quill until he once again encountered Porcupine. Not remembering that he had left it on the ground, Rhinoceros thought in panic that he must have swallowed it while using his mouth to sew. If this was the case, if he did indeed swallow the quill, it would come out as did all other things he swallowed. Promising Porcupine it would soon turn up, he began kicking his dung in search of it, as they all do to this day.[5]

Curiously, the one thing about the rhinoceros which these African stories wish to explain is his dung. This seems to indicate that it is these traces of rhino with which people were most familiar. Rhinos themselves must have been largely an absence in lives and cultures living so near their habitat. Still, a sense of stupidity runs throughout these tales from continental cohabitants. Even in religions which make profligate use of animals in their spiritual symbolism, rhinoceroses have remained outside iconography. Like western stories of the rhinoceros, these Asian and African tales employ rhino as a marginal character of bad temper, little brains, devoid of spiritual significance.

In centuries-old moralistic Jataka stories from India that tell of Buddha's presence in his former lives as part of the animal world, rhinoceroses occur only once. Even then, their role is only in the background, as just one among the native beasts who falsely believe the world is coming to an end after a hare hears the thump of fruit falling from a tree. A wise lion calms the stampeding group of oxen, lions, tigers, elephants, buffaloes, elk, deer, boar and rhinoceroses and discovers the source of the hare's inaccurate assumption. But the rhino here holds no meaning, other than as a representative of wild hysteria present in all the beasts, save the single lion, who represents Buddha in a former life.[6]

Perhaps this relative absence of rhinoceros symbolism in Indian culture is what encouraged Rudyard Kipling to imagine his own mythology. In his compilation of animal tales, *Just So Stories* (1902), Kipling attempts to explain the unusual look and bad behaviour of the rhinoceros but, like African and Asian tales, his rhino's actions are ineffective and, as Brunhoff's rhinos, result in making him look ridiculous. 'How the Rhinoceros got his Skin' begins with a native of India, a Parsee, baking a cake on an uninhabited island in the Red Sea. Just as the man was ready to eat, 'there came down to the beach from the Altogether Uninhabited Interior one Rhinoceros with a horn on his nose, two piggy eyes, and few manners'. This was not, explained Kipling, the animal as we know him today: 'In those days the Rhinoceros's skin fitted him quite tight. There were no wrinkles in it anywhere.' Despite the difference of his façade, however, 'he had no manners then, and he has no manners now, and he never will have any manners'.

The rhinoceros scares the Parsee away from his cake and the man ascends a palm tree. The rhino then comically spears the cake on his horn and, after devouring it, returns to the 'Exclusively Uninhabited Interior'. Five weeks later a heat wave arrived that was so intense 'everybody took off all the clothes they had'. The Rhinoceros removed his skin by unfastening the three buttons beneath his belly which held it together. Carrying it over his shoulder, he went back to the beach where he had previously stolen the Parsee's cake. He left his skin on the beach as he 'waddled straight into the water and blew bubbles through his nose'. Still sore that the rhinoceros had not apologized for his bad manners, the Parsee snuck onto the beach with his hat full of cake crumbs. He took the rhino's skin and rubbed it 'just as full of old, dry, stale, tickly cake-crumbs and some burned currants as ever it could *possibly* hold'.

When the rhinoceros came out of the water and buttoned on his skin it 'tickled like cake-crumbs in bed'. Scratching did no good, and he tried rolling on the sand, but still the crumbs tickled terribly. Then he rubbed against a palm tree 'so much and so hard that he rubbed his skin into a great fold over his shoulders, and another fold underneath, where the buttons used to be (but he rubbed the buttons off), and he rubbed some more folds over his legs . . . but it didn't make the least difference to the cake-crumbs'. His skin now ruined, 'he went home, very angry indeed and horribly scratchy; and from that day to this every rhinoceros has great folds in his skin and a very bad temper, all on account of the cake crumbs inside.'[7]

One of the problems of rhinoceroses in popular culture is their lack of voice. Very rarely do stories portray a talking rhino and, when they do, rhino words are few. In his reminiscences of working on Disney's animated version of Kipling's *The Jungle Book* (1967), animator Floyd Norman tells of a lost rhinoceros which exposes the perception that a talking rhinoceros is a ridiculous concept. Another animator was working on a storyboard for 'Rocky the Rhino', which was made into reels and screened for Walt Disney. The scenes were supposed to show Mowgli and Baloo on the way back from the village, encountering a 'dim-witted' rhino, voiced by comedian Frank Fontaine. Fontaine's signature 'idiotic laugh' did not entertain Disney, who 'shifted uncomfortably in his seat, and muttered under his breath'.

The rejected *Jungle Book* rhinoceros, Rocky.

Norman says that the scenes were drawn with humour but the voice ruined it. '[T]he sequence wasn't all that bad if you watched it with the sound turned off.' The trouble was imagining a voice for the rhinoceros. Instead of going back to casting, Disney doomed Rocky to non-existence: 'Walt was so annoyed by the moronic rhino that he wanted the beast cut from the picture.'[8]

Even Walt Disney – a man who seemed to be able to imagine words into the mouths of any creature – could not come to terms with a talking rhinoceros. In Disney's animated version of *Robin Hood* (1973) animals play the roles in the classic tale of charitable banditry. While the hero and his bride are portrayed as foxes, Prince John as a lion and Little John as a bear, the castle guards are vultures and rhinoceroses. The bipedal rhinos march military style in front of the prince's coach, accompanied by trumpeting elephants. Dressed in purple, with helmets and large spears, the one-horned rhinos look fiercely through intimidating red eyes.

Although one of this troop whistles flirtatiously at Little John who, dressed as a woman, has provocatively stashed the prince's gold into his dress, at no other point do the rhino soldiers talk. They are stout stalwarts of the prince, whose strength is undermined by their dim wits. When commanded to capture Robin Hood, they charge without direction and without stop-

This rhino guard whistles at Little John, a bear, dressed as a woman.

While this one comes close to beheading the hero, Robin Hood.

ping, comically ramming into rocks, trees and barred doors. Though violent, like Rataxes, Rocky and Kipling's rhino, the *Robin Hood* rhinos are ridiculous.

Kipling and Disney take the ridiculous sublime represented by Hemingway and employ it for comic relief. Whether trying

to explain its appearance or portray its violence these imagined rhinoceroses de-vilify the animal without making it any more appealing. When the imagined rhinoceros is removed from its native habitat, its natural behaviour seems bizarre. But imaginings of new rhinoceros behaviour, especially attempts to make it more human, seem just as ludicrous.

If an anthropomorphized rhino is ridiculous, what of a domesticated rhinoceros? Shel Silverstein portrays a pet rhinoceros in his children's book *Who Wants a Cheap Rhinoceros?* (1964), which imagines the many uses a boy could put such a pet to, for his own good, of course. Billed as 'sweet and fat and huggable', 'with floppy ears and cloppy feet, And friendly waggy tail', the rhino can stand between the boy and his parents when he wants money or doesn't want to get punished. The pet rhinoceros operates as a coat hanger, back scratcher, record player and report card eater. He appears dressed as a pirate and a crook, and his enormous bulk is apparently even good at games like hide and seek and jump rope.[9]

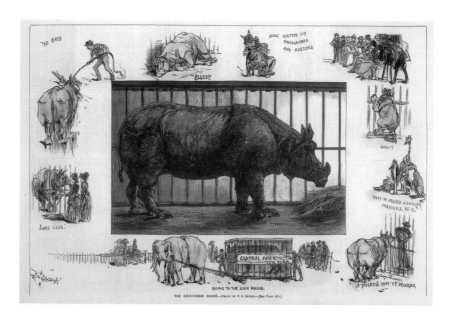

THE RHINOCEROS HORSE.—Drawn by F. S. Church.—[See Page 450.]

Barnum's comical vignettes.

The humour of Silverstein's tale lies in the absurdity of owning a pet rhinoceros, and attempting to teach it such tricks. A rhinoceros owned by famous American showman Phineas T. Barnum was ridiculous in its non-activity. An 1860 advertisement for the rhino in his menagerie depicted a cartoon collage entitled 'A Day in the Life of the Rhinoceros'. The scenes show a view from inside the animal's cage, giving a rhino-eye-view of his life. He is washed with a hose, lies around, sleeps and stands while women examine him from the other side of the bars. In another vignette, an elephant pulls the rhinoceros in its cage. The rhino is simply the recipient of gazes and the care of his keepers.

Gone are references to the unicorn, prehistoric beasts and 'paroxysms of rage'. Barnum's ad makes a mockery of rhinoceros sublimity by de-exoticizing the animal. The more human the portrayal, the more ridiculous the rhinoceros. The rhino here appears as mere amusement. Representing the lives of rhinoceroses in captivity, rather than in the wild, Barnum creates a completely cultural being. By taking the rhinoceros out of the wilderness, he also takes the wildness out of the rhinoceros.

And without wildness, what is a rhinoceros?

BEAUTIFUL

While Disney, Kipling and Silverstein imagine the wildness out of the rhinoceros, in seeking aesthetic pleasure some circuses force wildness back upon their tame rhinoceroses. An 1880s advertisement for a combined show of Barnum, the Great London Circus and Sanger's Royal British Menagerie depicts a completely monstrous-looking rhinoceros. As if to further testify to his character, the ground is littered with natives he has already trampled. Although an alluring advertisement for a rhinoceros circus act, if the rhino set to appear was truly this wild, it would not be in the circus to begin with.

So bent on re-wilding tame rhinos, circuses have even portrayed rhinos in unfamiliar contexts. One Mexican circus had a rhino act in which the animal was in its native skin, while the trainer was dressed as an ancient Mayan. The rhinoceros needs no uniform to make it exotic, but the one able to train such a wild animal must be exotic and ancient – even if that represents a culture which never lived alongside rhinoceroses. Like the natural history representations discussed earlier, aesthetically pleasing rhinoceroses have most often been ones represented as walking or wallowing in their native habitat. Contemporary photographer Britta Jaschinski, however, manages to convey rhino beauty in its form, not its surroundings. The graceful

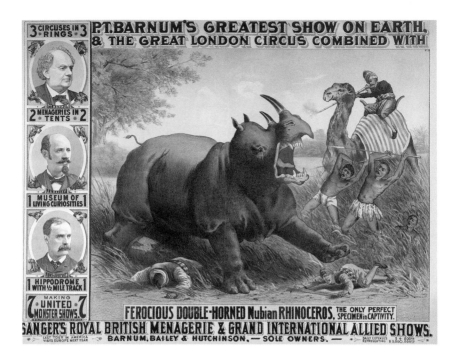

3 CIRCUSES IN 3
RINGS

P.T.BARNUM'S GREATEST SHOW ON EARTH,
& THE GREAT LONDON CIRCUS COMBINED WITH

2 MENAGERIES IN 2
TENTS

1 MUSEUM OF
LIVING CURIOSITIES 1

1 HIPPODROME
WITH ½ MILE TRACK 1

MAKING
7 UNITED 7
MONSTER SHOWS

FEROCIOUS DOUBLE-HORNED Nubian RHINOCEROS, THE ONLY PERFECT
SPECIMEN in CAPTIVITY.

SANGER'S ROYAL BRITISH MENAGERIE & GRAND INTERNATIONAL ALLIED SHOWS.
BARNUM, BAILEY & HUTCHINSON. — SOLE OWNERS. —

A promise of ferocity in the 1880s.

lines of rhino skin light up her portrait *Rhinoceros*, from the Wild Things series, in which the rhinoceros is set against no background at all. The sharp focus of the series' images has led many viewers to believe she used dead preserved animals to gain such stunning detail. In fact Jaschinski employed a mixture of zoo and wild animals in this series but, by erasing the background, succeeded in portraying only the animal. Free of context, the rhinoceros floats as *only* a rhinoceros. The viewer cannot say it is wild or captive, savage or tame, it is form alone.

Another of Jaschinski's rhinoceros photos shows one in a zoo enclosure, walking away from the camera's gaze. Unlike the charismatic enthusiasm of the Bronx Zoo's cover girl, Bessie, this rhino cares not for the photographer. It is not interested, curious or ready to charge. In what is possibly the first photograph ever taken of a rhinoceros, Frank Haes depicted a rhino at the London Zoo in 1864. Old Bet, as she was known, appears in her enclosure, looking out through the bars to the right of the frame. She seems peaceful, but Haes revealed that this scene was not a casual encounter. Because of the nature of photography at the time, in order to get a scene on film that would not blur from movement, it was necessary 'to run an animal about in its enclosure on a broiling hot day, endeavouring to tire him out, then rush off, shut yourself off in a closed tent to

Dalí faces his muse.

prepare your plate, coming out with eyes watering from the ether vapour, to find your subject refreshed from the interval of rest, and having to commence de novo, knowing that your plate was rapidly spoiling.' Haes's rhino portrait, however, shows none of this activity, capturing the rhino without motion.[10]

For Surrealist artist Salvador Dalí, the form of the rhinoceros represented not only beauty, but perfection. Concerned with neither gaze or behaviour, Dalí characteristically disassembles the rhinoceros. When presented with a gift of a rhinoceros horn, he was so taken with its form he exclaimed, 'This horn will save my life!' Dalí did not mean medicinally. The perfect spiral of the horn was a shape Dalí had been working with in his paintings for some thirty years. When he began to see rhino horns in his painting of Christ, he fell to his knees 'like a real madman'. He began to blatantly use the natural form in his work, painting his second *The Madonna of Port Lligat* and *Rhinoceros in Disintegration* in 1950 – the year of the gift.

Young Virgin Auto-Sodomized by the Horns of her Own Chastity (1954) is an erotic portrayal of disembodied rhino horns suggestively surrounding a naked woman. 'The rhinoceros horn is derived from the unicorn', Dalí wrote, 'the symbol of chastity . . . Paradoxically this painting which has an erotic appearance is the most chaste of all.' Dalí considered the rhino horn nature's perfection, which art must mimic – and like himself, artists had done so subconsciously. 'These horns', he explained, are 'the only ones in the animal kingdom constructed in accordance with a perfect logarithmic spiral . . . in Nature there has never been a more perfect example of a logarithmic spiral than the curve of the rhinoceros horn.' The logarithmic spiral maintains the same curve as it grows in size. Obsessed with this natural phenomenon, Dalí also praised the self-reproducing qualities of cauliflower.

Convinced that Vermeer's painting *The Lacemaker* was composed entirely of rhinoceros horns, Dalí copied the work hanging in the Louvre; his version was explicitly an explosion of horns. With photographer Robert Descharnes Dalí began an unfinished film, known as *The Prodigious History of the Lacemaker and the Rhinoceros*. For the film the pair visited Vincennes Zoo, where they filmed a rhinoceros, and encouraged it to charge a copy of Vermeer's painting (which it would not).[11]

Without even being seen on screen, rhinoceroses represent the ridiculous, the beautiful and the violent in one of the four cultural creations named for them – Eugène Ionesco's *Rhinocéros* (1959). This French Theatre of the Absurd play is interpreted as a critique of mass conformity to Fascism and Nazism during the Second World War. Ionesco designed a rhinoceros mask used in the original staging of the play, but when made into a film in 1974 no rhino props were employed.

Exaggerated colours lend beauty to this illustration of a white and an Indian rhinoceros.

Instructions on how to draw a rhinoceros, painted on a cigarette box.

Directed by Tom O'Horgan, starring Zero Mostel, Gene Wilder and Karen Black, the story tells the absurd tale of human beings changing into rhinoceroses. Although not a single rhinoceros image is shown on screen, the audience knows they are in the presence of rhinoceroses by relentless bellowing, crashing and stampeding. Unlike the more amusing rhinos of Barnum, Disney, Silverstein and Kipling, Ionesco's wild rhinoceroses represent an absurd counterpoint to civilization – a ridiculous sublime.

The first rhino appears as it comes running down the street outside a restaurant, kicking up a cloud of dust. Later it crashes into the restaurant and kills a cat. All of this violence is represented by things breaking, dust swirling, noises from the crash and the rhino himself. This rhinoceros turns out to be Stanley's coworker; his wife recognizes him because of the glasses he is wearing. He destroys the stairs to the office, whether in an attempt to simply get to work, or a ploy to destroy his coworkers, we do not know. But one thing is for sure, as the boss articulates, 'he is definitely fired for good'.

In the central scene of the film John is slowly turning into a rhinoceros, while Stanley watches. John, seemingly oblivious to what is happening to him, criticizes the coworker for allowing himself to turn into an animal. 'He obviously enjoyed turning into a rhinoceros. Or he would have resisted it,' reasons John even as he compulsively stomps his foot. 'It's just not normal', pleads Stanley, 'for a human being to turn into a dumb animal'. Perhaps growing more aware of what is happening to him, and perhaps enjoying the beginnings of what it feels like to be an animal, John explains, 'It's not as bad as all that. After all, rhinoceroses are living creatures too.' The conversation continues:

> *Stanley*: Well don't you think that there's a little difference in the mentality?

John: Are you under the impression that our way of life is superior?

Stanley: No but I think that we have a few moral standards which might conflict with the standards of these animals.

John: I'm sick of you and your moral standards.

Stanley: Well what do you put in their place?

John: Nature. The laws of nature. (Bellows.)

Stanley: The laws of nature can lead to the laws of the jungle.

John: That would suit me fine. Just fine.

Stanley: Yes you say that but I know that deep down you don't believe it.

John: We must build our lives a new foundation. Must get back to primeval integrity.

With this, the conversation pauses. John kisses a painting of Richard Nixon hanging on his wall. 'I don't agree with you at all', concludes Stanley. I don't know what to think about the alignment of rhinoceros politics with Nixon, but this conversation clearly reveals Ionesco's alignment of rhinoceroses with the most primitive form of being. The people who turn into rhinoceroses are sick of civilization and of selfhood. We know John has gone over to the other side when he catches his reflection in the mirror and, not recognizing his own image, charges. Meanwhile, Stanley holds on to his individuality pointlessly until the end. Looking at his reflection, he sees a 'monster' and wishes for a horn and smooth brow to better define his features, and thicker skin instead of his soft human flesh. The formerly ugly rhinoceros is now the ideal to which his aesthetic aspires.

What is most interesting about Ionesco's work is how he imagined it might feel to turn into a rhinoceros. Through the character of John, we experience the human turning animal. Speech gives way to blurts and bellows. He feels an excess of uncontrollable energy and heat. Aroused by Stanley's conversation, he begins to charge towards him rather than argue back. Another human-turning-rhino, Norman, discovers a distaste for meat accompanied by a desire to go outside and eat on the grass.

Now the minority, the remaining humans try to figure out what to do with the rhinos. They argue over whether the animals have a language and if they should try to understand it. The last humans left, Daisy and Stanley, split solutions. Daisy looks out at the rhino herd longingly, 'They look happy, not insane', she says. 'They look normal. They were right to do what they did.' Compared with human weakness and 'this morbid feeling' of love, Daisy falls for 'the ardor and the tremendous energy that emanates from those creatures'.

TOUGH

Ionesco plays with the idea that a rhinoceros can only be perceived as beautiful if everything else in the world was more rhinoceros-like. Daisy's early assertion that a rhinoceros is 'a big, ugly animal', rings truer with the majority of rhino representation in cultures around the globe than does her later love for the creatures. There are some cultural spaces, however, where the 'tremendous energy' and toughness of rhinoceroses is appreciated, not vilified. When aligned with objects of human technological achievement, rhinoceros toughness becomes a thing of beauty.

In front of Paris's Palais du Trocadéro, animal sculptor Henri Alfred Jacquemart created a bronze menagerie consisting of a horse, a bull, an elephant and a rhinoceros for the Paris Exposition of 1878. The sight of his dramatically posed rhinoceros juxtaposed against the Eiffel Tower caught the imagination of a number of artists and photographers who portrayed the short, dense rhino with its horn reaching upwards in front of the sleek lightness of the tower. Jules Ernest Renoux's painting is one of the more notable representations of this work. The statue itself now stands outside the Musée d'Orsay.[12]

But the rhino–technology complex goes back even further. The 1830 rhinoceros discussed earlier was said to 'resist the force of a musket ball'. Even as Theodore Roosevelt mourned the rhinoceros's inability to stand up to modern technology, he used it as the ultimate test of the power and effectiveness of his guns. Even Brunhoff's Rataxes is tested against the power of dynamite. Similarly, Hergé's colonialist boy-hero Tintin meets a rhinoceros who masters the gun. In *Tintin in the Congo* (1946) a rhinoceros obliviously wanders near a tree where Tintin is taking a rest from his camera safari. His rifle hangs from a branch, and the rhinoceros tangles his horn on its strap. The rhino's thoughts are expressed with only a question mark in a cartoon bubble. The rhino starts thrashing about and the gun falls to the ground, letting off a shot that pierces Tintin's hat. 'He may not have good eyesight', exclaims Tintin's dog Snowy, 'but he certainly can shoot'. Frightened by the result of his own clumsiness, the rhino runs away.[13]

In contemporary culture, rhinos posed with technological objects are more often used to sell the technology by visually equating rhino toughness with product durability. A popular advertisement seen almost monthly in *National Geographic* magazine during 2006 shows a sturdy looking rhinoceros, half in shadow, his face in the sun, ears alertly turned forward, and eye looking just left of the unseen photographer. Next to the image is a checklist, with all boxes checked: pith helmet, cargo shorts, running shoes and Pentax's K100D camera. Below the

image the camera is featured, much smaller than the rhino, proclaiming its light weight and shake reduction feature 'Essential to the experience'. So we are to assume the checklist indicates other necessities: shorts with pockets to carry the camera; pith helmet supposedly to protect against the rhino; and running shoes to try to get away from it.

The rhino's inability to resist technology was sometimes ignored in the desire to compare the two. 'There he was', wrote Ernest Hemingway upon spotting a rhinoceros in Africa, 'long-hulked, heavy-sided, prehistoric looking, the hide like vulcanized rubber.' Lang described the use of the horn: 'acts as a fender in thrusting aside obstructions in the jungle'. Like the rhinos in *Hatari* who duel with jeeps, the toughness of rhino hide and its natural strength are qualities automobile companies exploit to make a sale. Spare tyre covers on Land Rovers feature a rhinoceros, as does a decal from England showing a sport utility vehicle driving over a rhino's back. The rhino is so strong it is unaffected by the load, and the car so powerful it can overcome this odd obstacle.[14]

A 1951 advertising campaign for Armstrong Tires announced its brand's 'exclusive Rhino-Flex construction' and guaranteed its tyre against eighteen months worth of road hazards. An ad in the *Saturday Evening Post* on 25 August of that year features a huge rhino standing on its hind legs, leaning nonchalantly on a case containing the tyres. He smokes a cigar and wears a cap. He indeed looks tough – in attitude as well as exterior covering – as the headline boldly announces 'NONE TOUGHER!' By conflating the two meanings of 'tough' Armstrong Tires sold its product to an audience interested in the product's resiliency as well as, perhaps, their own identification of the coolness of the gangster-esque rhinoceros in the ad.[15]

Today there are garbage cans that are 'Rhino Tough'. A rhinoceros with a handle stands as the symbol for a company that makes heavy duty cases for transporting audio equipment. In another seeming conflation of toughness and coolness there is an independent record label named Rhino Records and the trendy *ecko unltd clothing company, which employs the rhinoceros as its logo, featuring it prominently on most of its clothing. The company's founder, Marc Ecko, uses the popularity of his rhinoceros image to help out real rhinos. He has pledged financial support to help double populations of black, Indian and Sumatran rhinoceroses in consort with the International Rhino Foundation. The San Diego Zoo's Wild Animal Park even named a new baby in 2005 after the designer-entrepreneur.[16]

When not a symbol of toughness, contemporary rhino imagery speaks to quite the opposite quality of rhinos – their precipitous existence. As an icon of wildlife conservation the rhinoceros symbolizes a species that has met with some success, but whose future existence is far from secure. The profile

In this bumper sticker, the truly tough rhinoceros takes the hit of an SUV.

"NONE TOUGHER!"

UNCONDITIONALLY GUARANTEED!

Smart motorists demand tough tires these days. And Armstrong tires are *so* tough they're *unconditionally guaranteed* for 18 *months against all road hazards!* Exclusive Rhino-Flex construction—plus 38 years' experience in building better passenger, truck and tractor tires—makes this amazing guarantee possible. See your nearby dealer displaying the famous Armstrong "Tuffy." *Armstrong Rubber Company, West Haven 16, Conn., Norwalk, Conn., Natchez, Miss., Des Moines, Iowa, 605 Market Street, San Francisco, Calif. Export Division: 20 East 50th St., New York 22, N. Y.*

ARMSTRONG Rhino-Flex TIRES

Species Survival Plan ·

American
Zoological
Association logo
for their Species
Survival Plan.

The Save the
Rhino logo.

of a mother and baby rhino is the chosen icon for the American Zoo Association's Species Survival Plan – a programme in which zoos collaborate to diversify the gene pool of their captive endangered animals. An organization dedicated to rhino conservation, Save the Rhino, uses a bold stamp in which the rhino is outlined – its front in white, its back half in black. This icon seems to be revealing the uncertain lives of rhinos today – half in light, half in dark – as well as their multifarious cultural image. With a long legacy of bad behaviour, the rhino has a long way to go before it can claim the white hat of the good guy. Its survival is at stake, however, in this ability to transform its image.

Tyres as strong as
a rhino's hide.

From Andy Warhol
and Kurt
Benirschke's
Vanishing Animals
(1986).

5 Horns, Habits and Habitats

'But the rhino's greatest misfortune is that he carries a
fortune on his nose.'
Lee M. Talbot (1959)[1]

In 1920 Herbert Lang reported the demand for white rhinoceros horn in northern Africa was evidence of 'greasy and sleek
humanity'. In addition to Asians using powder for 'supersti-
tious' medicine, Lang cited a 'craze among native chiefs' to
fashion staffs of the longest rhino horns. Implicating his own
cultural heritage, he denounced the European and American
desire for decorative canes, cups and amulets made of horn,
and tables made of rhino hide which add 'to the pride of the
home owned by men of the colonial set'. Even industry was to
blame for the loss of rhinos, as hide was used in machinery as
a durable lathe.[2]

Valued for its unique lustre when carved and its healing
properties when powdered, the rhinoceros's horn has been the
Achilles heel of the species. In one of the world's most ecologi-
cally unsustainable extraction industries, animals weighing
1300 kg or more are killed for a few kilograms of keratin – the
fibrous strands of hair of which the horn is composed. The illegal trade of horn has flourished despite decades of regulation
from local governments, global political pressure, and international conservation efforts. Whether blaming a fashion craze,
superstition or human corruption, the ups and downs of rhinoceros populations have manufactured a perilous existence for
one of the world's largest creatures.

Horn removed, a rhino body is left to decay.

DAGGERS AND DRUGS

In the eyes of Asian culture, writes Richard Ellis, the rhinoceros is a 'walking apothecary' thought to cure just about everything except the very thing it is most rumoured to cure – impotency. The idea that rhino horn (*xi jiao*) is an aphrodisiac does not appear in any traditional Chinese medical literature and appears to be a myth spread by westerners. In 1987 biologist E. B. Martin reported that in northern India, Thailand and Burma rhino blood, urine and penises were consumed as aphrodisiacs, but indicates that this use spread from East Africa to Asia with conservationists. Another conservationist, Eric Dinerstein, calls the aphrodisiac rumours a creation of the media and claims that in Asia in 2003 many perceive this as 'a kind of anti-Chinese hysteria'.[3]

In Traditional Chinese Medicine (TCM) the powdered horn is used to treat a variety of ills. In one of the field's standard texts, *Pen Ts'ao Kang Mu* (1597), Li Shih-chen advised against rhino horn being taken by pregnant women as it may kill the foetus. *Xi*

Horn and
packaged
medicine made
from it.

jiao is classed as a 'heat-clearing, blood-cooling' medicine and is used to cure the following: poisoning, devil possession, jasmine and snake poisoning, hallucinations and 'bewitching nightmares', typhoid, headache, fever, carbuncles, boils, delirium, fear, anxiety, upset liver, blurry vision, excess of phlegm, convulsions, dysentery, vomiting, drug overdose, arthritis, melancholia, sore throat, haemorrhage, nose and rectal bleeding, smallpox and 'the evil miasma of hill streams'. The abundance of cures provided by the rhino horn proves it is no frivolous component of traditional Chinese medical practice.[4]

While TCM practitioners believe the uniqueness of the rhino horn has no substitute, sceptical western medical practitioners have tested the chemical consistency of the horn, and claim that its difference from buffalo horn is minimal. In 1996 Wiseman and Ellis wrote in *Fundamentals of Traditional Chinese Medicine* that buffalo horn could easily be used as a substitute for rhino horn. Tests in western medical labs have looked for their fever-reducing qualities, but studies have proven inconclusive. The demand for rhino horn in traditional medicine threatens relics of China's own past. Recycled rhinoceros horn carvings from the Ming (1368–1644) and Ching (1644–1912) dynasties are scooped up by drug factories and piled in warehouses to meet future *xi jiao* demand.[5]

The earliest carvings of rhino horn date to first-century China, where decorative bowls and cups were used to detect poison. Modern experiments reveal that the alkaloids in certain poisons do react visibly with the keratin in the horn. In India the horn is believed to detect poison and ease childbirth if placed under the bed. In addition to horn, rhino urine is hung in doorways intending to keep away evil spirits and sickness.

Containers made from rhino feet.

Martin reported that zoos there offer rhino urine from their captive animals to guests who request it, and who believe it heals sore throats, prevents asthma attacks, and, if hung in the doorway, keeps away sickness and evil spirits.[6]

Although *xi jiao* is an Asian tradition, African as well as Asian rhinos have been victims of the practice. While Asian horn is preferred by TCM practitioners for its superior 'cooling' properties, poachers in Africa have made a lucrative trade with Asian dealers. The illegal trade flows closer to home, as well. In the Middle East, rhino horn is in demand, not for its healing properties, but its beauty. In Yemen and Oman elegantly carved dagger handles, called jambiyas, symbolize the status and masculinity of their owners. Rhino horn is the desired medium because of its amber translucency, durability, and development of a desired patina with age and use.

When the Middle East became the oil centre of the world, during the 1970s, an increase in local wealth increased demand for horn. African horn was preferred, as there is less waste in the carving process. One horn dealer reportedly produced 6,000 jambiya a year. In 1980 jambiya were being sold for as

Jambiya worn on the belt as a sign of status.

much as $11,000. In the 1990s jambiya were in much smaller demand. In addition to economic decline in Yemen, an Islamic edict declared rhino killing against the will of Islam. New materials were used for jambiya, though there remains illegal trade and sale of those with rhino horn handles.

The horn industry grew in war-torn Africa. The easy availability of guns along with inability of weak or overthrown governments made places like Uganda, Chad, Ethiopia, Somalia, Zaire and Angola ripe for unseen killings and illegal trade. Many people displaced by unsettled times found rhino horn a ready source of money on the run. Some situations were so dire that during Uganda's War of Liberation in the 1970s the second to last white rhinoceros in the entire region was killed – for meat. Although the instances of rhino killing for subsistence are few, in war-torn countries a dead endangered animal has little significance alongside endangered human lives.

Despite laws protecting Africa's white and black rhinoceros populations, the deadliest decades for them were the 1970s and '80s. In Kenya, for example, the black rhinoceros population recovered from the damaging effects of early twentieth-century sport hunting only to fall dramatically, by 80 per cent, in the 1970s. Even in parks life was no more assured. Meru National Park lost a full 90 per cent of its population at this time, due almost entirely to poaching.[7]

Although sometimes begun in relative innocence or desperation, rhinoceros poaching has grown through the second half of the twentieth century into a dark and mysterious industry. Rhino are not the only victims – the same men who seek horn also kill elephants for ivory. It is not the poachers themselves that are the problem, reveals Australian-born photographer Patrick Brown, who is one of the few non-participants to have seen the innards of this industry. Documenting the illegal

A muddy rhinoceros at peace.

wildlife trade in Asia, Brown found sympathy for the motivations of many poachers who often began out of simple need to provide for their families. With generations of hunters in their ancestral history, hunting seemed an obvious, unproblematic, way to pull themselves from the claws of poverty. The real problem, claims Brown, is the middlemen and salesmen who encourage trade and create demand, along with government officials who turn a blind eye as their pockets grow deep with payoffs.[8]

WHAT IS A RHINO GOOD FOR?

Although rhino horn is valued for healing properties and as an object of beauty and status, in its raw state upon the rhino's head it seems to have little value at all. Without a history of being valued for their helpfulness to humans while alive rhinos became easy and guilt-free targets for those seeking not only subsistence, but fortunes. Beyond the horn, the body of the rhino has found little value. There are unsubstantiated reports of Asians and Africans eating rhinoceros meat during the nineteenth century, but it was never a staple of any human diet. Nor have rhinoceroses found their way into spirituality. Despite assigning roles to all manner of animals in their iconography including elephants, monkeys, cattle and snakes, Asian cultures have largely left rhinoceroses out of the picture. Only in death have they been valued.

There is but one ritual, of a small Hindu sect in Nepal, in which rhinos are used as part of a sacred rite called the Blood Tarpan. Believing the horn of the rhino to be a gift from Lord Vishnu, each Nepalese king must sacrifice a rhinoceros upon his accession. Martin describes this ritual as practised in the Chitwan Valley, the region's only remaining rhinoceros habitat. When a rhino is found it is killed and disembowelled. The king then sits inside the carcass – bloody up to his waist – and offers up rhino blood libations to the Hindu gods in memory of his parents. The meat is given away, save for a piece between the hoof and ankle of one leg, which the king consumes.

Although the Blood Tarpan takes the life of a rhinoceros, it is a symbolic and sacrificial killing, central to the king's ability to rule. This special significance of the rhinoceros has, argued Martin, resulted in its protection. The Chitwan Valley has long been a refuge for rhinos, and they remain protected by armed guards. Here, where rhinoceroses fill a symbolic role central to the culture, its rulers and its religion, they are preserved.[9]

The lack of spiritual space for the rhinoceroses in local and international cultures has contributed more than a little to its endangerment. Endowed with no godly significance and no usefulness during life, rhinoceroses are objectified commodities. The problem of the international conservation movement then, is to give people a reason to keep rhinos around. Rhino conservation struggles to cast this odd animal in a new iconography. Conservation of wild animals relies upon the creation of new meanings – some might even say, new mythologies – with global appeal.

Through his photographs, Patrick Brown tells a story not only of the odd and brutal illegal animal trade, but of how this trade influences local, regional, and global events. 'Even if one less rhino gets killed', he says, 'at least it might have done something.' His greatest desire for his photos is to influence the thoughts of those who do not already sympathize with the plight of endangered wildlife – those in the 'developing world' who have more influence over practices in their own countries where the rhinos reside. He hopes an exhibition of his photos in a public space 'shocks as many people as possible and brings them to their senses'.[10]

Media coverage on the unsteady fate of rhinoceroses often argues for the end of poaching by laying out graphic photographs of rhino slaughter. Instead of appealing to audiences with scenes of aesthetically pleasing rhinos, or attempting to make rhinos cute, conservationists expose human brutality. Piles of disembodied horns suggest unstoppable greed. By saving the rhinoceros, they argue, we are saving ourselves from our own brutal nature and savage greed. To paraphrase American nineteenth-century nature writer and proto-conservationist Henry David Thoreau's rhetoric on wildness: in the preservation of rhinoceroses/wildness, lies the preservation of the world.

Does the continued existence of rhinoceroses serve only to prove our own morality? While there are ecological reasons for maintaining the diversity of life on earth, most conservation literature calls upon sympathy to motivate the masses. The state of wildlife conservation has reached a precipitous point for many species. It is a frightening fact that the future existence of rhinoceroses is entirely dependent upon the will of humans. Rhinos must find another way to carry their fortune – off their noses.

Conservationists are convinced that ecotourism has the potential to bring in sources of money and employment that would cull poaching. But at the going price of $5,000 per kilogram, convincing poachers to give up their trade seems unlikely. While Brown sings the praises of park rangers who put their lives on the line standing up to poachers, their diminutive pay of $10 to $25 a month cannot compare to the money promised poachers. Although he calls such men the 'unknown soldier[s]' of wars for wildlife, conservationists have little but words and sentiment to lure locals away from the illegal trade. At the high prices demanded for the horn, biologist Lee M. Talbot argued in 1956, 'the wonder is not that rhinos were rare by 1900 but that they still existed at all.'[11]

While the Middle East has lessened its desire for rhino horn jambiyas, Asian markets continue to require *xi jiao*. In the 1980s economists estimated that 3,000 rhinos would have to be killed to fulfil the demand for the three to four kilograms of horn per animal. Although the demand for ivory threatens elephants in the same region, probably tracked by the same poachers who seek rhinoceroses, the complex social structure and superior adaptability of the larger animal has made them better able to protect themselves. 'Removal of a part of its [rhino's] habitat is tantamount to removing a part of its population. In fact, the rhino serves as a good example of an animal whose survival is completely dependent on the will of man.'[12]

In addition to calling upon the dark side of humanity reflected through rhino poaching, conservationists attempt to reconstruct the animal's public image. This monumental task seeks to overcome their centuries-old association with a sort of savage wildness that, while often seen as sublime, has not been something many

Greater One-Horned Rhino	2.0m
White Rhino	1.5m
Black Rhino	1.0m
Javan Rhino	0.5m
Sumatran Rhino	0.0m

Comparison of rhino sizes.

wish to preserve. By turning the tables to represent poachers as the source of senseless wildness, conservationists hope to redeem the rhinoceros. But its image as an inevitably dying creature maintains a strong hold on the imagination. Just as Theodore Roosevelt mourned the demise of the prehistoric rhinoceros, as late as 1980 conservationist–biologist Edward R. Ricciuti described the rhino as 'a zoological museum piece, a holdover from times long past, a loner that is unadaptable and rather stupid'.[13]

SPECIES STATUS

In 1994 the US Congress passed the Tiger and Rhinoceros Conservation Act, declaring that since 1970 the global rhinoceros population had declined by 90 per cent. The Act threatened restricted trade with Taiwan and China if they did not take action against the illegal trade of rhino horn, and pledged funds to assist conservation efforts. Although seventeen years earlier CITES (Convention on International Trade in Endangered Species of Flora and Fauna) banned the trade of rhino products, poaching has continued. The survival of remaining rhinoceros populations has become an international project, involving pressure from conservationists, cooperation of local governments and compliancy of local populations.

Wildlife biologists investigate the lives and needs of each rhinoceros population to better understand how to manage land, animals and people. All rhinoceroses face similar threats to survival, but each species and subspecies has specific characteristics, habits and habitats which have affected their history of human contact and encounter. With humans as their only known predator, encounters in the wild can be unpredictable and elusive. 'It is a slow job learning about the rhinoceros' lifestyle', asserts biologist Andrew Laurie, 'I spent hours watching while they did nothing'. Although even those most intimate with rhino lives admit it is a difficult animal to understand, biologists do their best to construct wild rhino lives.[14]

Biologists now class existing rhinoceroses into five species – two in Africa, three in Asia. Their observations record the differences and similarities amongst the species and subspecies. Rhinos around the world share poor eyesight and a reliance upon smell and hearing to interpret their world and to perceive imminent dangers. Thus they are all prone to charging with some uncertainty about the threat posed by an unfamiliar presence. All rhinos spend a great deal of time wallowing in muddy areas or waterholes. This activity regulates their body temperature and removes parasites from their skin. Communication between rhinos is achieved by scent marking with urine, dung and foot scraping, which releases a liquid from foot glands. Vocalizations are employed by all rhinos to a varying degree, with white rhinoceroses the most vocal, possessing a range of noises from wails to snarls to squeaks. Such noises are used by calves to get attention from their mothers, during mating, when injured and – as in the case of the black rhino's distinctive puffing snort – when alarmed.

Biologists, however, do more than contribute to literature on rhinoceros behaviour. They analyse the effects of human behavior on rhinoceroses, and hope to reach a balance between the interests of the two parties. The behaviour which interests biologists revolves around life processes and needs for specific environmental conditions. They are interested in what will help rhinoceroses survive in the wild, not in their own human–animal encounters. They are as interested in differences as they are in similarities, and have compiled representations of each rhinoceros species which reveal not so subtle differences about their habits and habitats. Although clearly the best way to map out wildlife and land management practices, this information is, as we have seen, not the only influential representation of rhinoceroses and their behaviour. For successful conservation, the problems of cultural construction must be addressed alongside the problems of environmental conditions.

WHITE RHINOCEROS

The erroneously named white rhinoceros (*Ceratotherium simum*) is one conservation success story. Known more accurately as the square-lipped rhinoceros, the confusion began with a misinterpretation of the Dutch word for the species 'wiyd'. Although the word means 'wide', English colonialists heard this as 'white' and the name stuck. Its skin, however, is much the same hue as the black rhinoceros, though both often take on the colour of whatever soil they are coating their hides with in mud wallows.

Ceratotherium means 'horned beast' (*cerato* for horn, *therium* for beast). The species name, *simum*, is Greek for 'flat-nosed,' after the white rhino's wide mouth, which allows it to graze on the shortest of grasses. At 1,800–2,700 kilograms, white rhinos are the largest land animals after elephants, standing 1.5–1.8

metres tall and 3.8–5 metres long. Their skin is yellowish brown
to slate grey, with some hair fringing its ears and tail. There is a
hump on the back of the neck which supports its heavy head and
two horns; the anterior usually measures 94–201 cm, though it
can grow much longer in the northern subspecies. In comparison, the posterior is a mere 55 cm in length.

White rhino cows give birth to a single calf about every two
to three years, with gestation lasting sixteen months. Sexual
maturity is reached earlier by females, at six years of age, while
males do not mature until at least ten years old. Females are
rarely seen alone, congregating with other females and sub-
adults, while males tend to be more solitary and territorial.
Their preferred habitat has a mixture of short grass savannah
with the shade of dense bush and water holes for drinking and
wallowing. Their days are spent eating, sleeping and wallowing
in mud or dust to rid their skin of parasites and to keep cool.
White rhinos are said to be more shy and less aggressive than
other rhinos and live at most 50 years.

The northern (*C. s. cottoni*) is the rarer of the two subspecies,
remaining only in the Democratic Republic of the Congo. Not

long after the expeditions of Roosevelt and Lang, two parks were established to protect them in the late 1930s – Garamba National Park (DRC) and Southern National Park (Sudan). Since this time, however, the horn trade has returned their status to small numbers. Additionally, civil wars have prevented sufficient government protection and expanded the availability of weapons. In 1998 there were 25 individuals. A recent conservation effort was proposed to airlift ten northern whites from Garamba to a preserve in Kenya in 2005, but the Congolese government prevented the effort.

Southern white rhino (*C. s. simum*) counts in southern Africa stand at 13,000, making it the most abundant subspecies of rhino in the world. Why the two subspecies of white rhinoceros live in such widely separated regions is something of a mystery. The only evidence of their existence between the

White rhinoceros at San Diego Wild Animal Park.

two current ranges is cave paintings and fossil finds from the last ice age, during which it is likely their range was split. Their genetic differences are much greater than the variation among black rhino subspecies.

By the end of the nineteenth century southern white rhinos numbered only twenty animals. Nearly a hundred years of protection has brought their numbers to respectable amounts. By the end of the 1990s 8,440 animals resided in over 200 separate locations; 650 lived in captivity. The recovery of the southern whites, now the most numerous of all rhino, is the biggest success story in rhinoceros conservation. On the brink of extinction in the 1920s, the Republic of South Africa implemented a captive-conservation programme and revived the population from fewer than a hundred to 7,500 individuals. Additionally, wild-caught southern white rhinos will breed in captivity; 91 calves have been born at San Diego Wild Animal Park since 1972, though the rate of reproduction among those born in captivity is low.[15]

In KwaZulu-Natal, Hluhlowe-Umfolozi white rhinos are bred and auctioned to private landowners at up to £50,000 per animal. These bidders are banking on the rhino to bring in crowds of photo safari-seekers, wishing to see 'wild' rhinoceros. But when a species is so dependent upon humans for their existence, and placed in entirely new environments for the specific purpose of tourism, do they retain their wildness?

BLACK RHINOCEROS

Black rhinos (*Diceros bicornis*) were more adaptable to changes in habitat and climate than their continental neighbours. They survive quite well in dry, cool forest or grassland, while whites suffer when removed from their grassland and savannah woods. Reputed to be less aggressive than Africa's black rhinos, white rhinos were also easier targets for hunters and poachers. But the advantage of instilling more fear and better ecological adaptability have not helped black rhinos fare any better.

Over 100,000 black rhinos lived throughout much of Africa in the 1800s, making it the most populous of all rhinos. Even into the twentieth century this species was the most plentiful of all the world's rhinos. In 1900 there were several hundred thousand in Africa. Hunting exterminated most of these animals, leaving only 110 in southern Africa by 1933. In addition to sport hunting, rhino were shot to make way for agricultural production. In Kenya a game control programme took 1,000 rhinos in just two years. Although no official count existed until 1980, it is thought that in 1960 about 100,000 black rhino remained on the continent, after which poaching caused a dramatic decline throughout the 1970s, leaving no more than 15,000 in 1981.

The Asian and Middle Eastern demand for horn increased through the 1970s and '80s. Coupled with political unrest, rhinos suffered from a lack of protection, and poachers easily culled 96 per cent of the black rhino population by 1992. A 2003 count for the species stood at 3,610 and on 7 July 2006 the IUCN announced the subspecies West African black rhinoceros (*Diceros bicornis longipes*) tentatively extinct.

Much smaller than Africa's white rhinoceros, the black rhinoceros can be distinguished by a lack of shoulder hump, small skulls and ears, and pronounced forehead. The most distinguishing difference between the black and white rhinos is the black's pointed prehensile upper lip for grasping leaves and twigs. As a browser, it has access to a greater variety of food than grazers, eating 220 different species of plants. This varied diet helps it adapt to new environments, and reduces woody plants leaving more grasses for other animals. Black rhinos can

Black rhinoceros.

reach a weight of 800–1,400 kilograms. Their bodies are roughly 2.86–3.05 metres in length and 1.4–1.6 metres tall, while their horns range from 0.5–1.3 m long in the anterior, and 2–55 cm high in the posterior.

They live shorter lives than white rhinos, averaging 30–35 years in the wild; in captivity they tend to survive an additional ten years. Births occur about every three years, and gestation is the same as for whites at sixteen months. Some females may reach maturity as early as four years of age, while males range between seven and ten years. Females are less gregarious than their white counterparts, but do exist peacefully in overlapping territory. Males are solitary, and their territorial behaviour is still not completely understood, though fights over land often result in the death of young and old males. Black rhinos appear more aggressive when startled than most rhinos, and fear of adult males often drives newly independent calves to seek protection of other females once their mother has encouraged them to move on at two to four years of age. These sub-adults have even been known to accompany white rhino females in the wild. Mothers will sometimes accept their calf back after they have been on their own for a few months.

Of the four subspecies, the south-central (*D. b. minor*) is the most numerous and resides in central Tanzania and south through Zambia, Zimbabwe and Mozambique, and in northern and eastern South Africa. The south-western subspecies (*D. b. bicornis*) is adapted to the arid and semi-arid savannahs of Namibiam southern Angola, western Botswana and western South Africa. The range of the east African (*D. b. michaeli*) black rhino has been greatly reduced from Sudan, Ethopia, Somalia and Kenya to its only remaining habitat in Tanzania. The west African black rhinoceros – if any remain at all – resides in northern Cameroon.[16]

Oddly, conservation efforts resemble the practices they seek to put an end to. Shot with tranquillizer darts from the sky, black rhinos were the subjects of an ambitious experiment to preemptively remove their valuable horns. By doing so, conservationists hoped poachers would then leave the animals alone. Infuriated, poachers killed the rhinos anyway. Rhinos were similarly shot with tranquillizer darts in the 1960s to relocate them to the protected borders of national parks.[17]

But park boundaries did not ensure protection – even for specimens who had gained some celebrity. Gladys and Gertie were two black rhinos residing in the Amboseli Game Reserve in the 1950s. Tourists flocked to the foothills of Mount Kilimanjaro to photograph these two relatively friendly rhinoceroses. Even after they lost their horns in 1959, they continued to be one of Kenya's top attractions. In January of 1962

Black rhinoceros being relocated.

Gladys was killed by poachers. The act was disparaged as cowardly and cruel.[18]

Even Hugh and Jane Stanton's beloved clown, Cora, was not free from the fate that befell many African rhinos. Cora was found dead, her horn removed, the obvious victim of poachers. In fact the fate of many of the rhinos on Bushwacker's 130-square-kilometre sanctuary met the same fate. During the 1960s if rhino were not poached they were squeezed out of the region by squatters who moved in along the Kibwezi River. Without government regulation of squatters or game, Bushwhackers' 25 rhino surely met their ends. Even protection cannot secure the survival of rhinoceroses.[19]

Their struggle with poachers is just as difficult as their struggle with their public image. In the 1960s conservation biologist C.A.W. Guggisberg blamed the temper of the black rhino for its long history as a hunting target. Since 1685, he argued, when

Dutch governor Simon van der Stel's carriage was upturned by a charging black rhino, people have perceived the animal's charges as a threat. They reported the animal making its way undeterred through lines of porters and oxen, and even going after cars and trains. Their reputation as 'dangerous' caused shooting upon sight.[20]

When rhinos were contained within national park boundaries, however, Guggisberg writes, humans discovered its true nature. It is 'a very pathetic prehistoric creature, quite unable to adapt itself to modern times'. With this knowledge, Guggisberg disparaged rhino hunting: 'it can, after all, be killed as easily as a cow, and who would like to have himself photographed grinning inanely over a cow he has shot?' Conservation support depends entirely on perceptions of the animal. If there is no heroics in hunting, assumes Guggisberg, the sport hunters will leave it alone.[21]

Even as he calls for saving the black rhino, and for understanding its true nature, Guggisberg falls into the trap of the rhino's public image: 'It is our duty to save and preserve this short-tempered, prehistorically stupid but nevertheless so immensely lovable creature.' Those who wish the rhino well, and who think it lovable, still cannot separate themselves from the prehistoric and mean-spirited image embedded in our culture.[22]

INDIAN RHINOCEROS

In areas where Marco Polo easily observed his 'unicorns', as early as 1908 Indian rhinoceroses (*Rhinoceros unicornis*) were relegated to just two valleys along the Brahmaputra River. The double threat of over-hunting (for sport and for trade) and loss of habitat due to new agricultural enterprises such as teak plantations and an expanding human population brought rhinos to

A park sign in India warns of rhino sightings.

the brink of extinction. Even where they could seek refuge, rhinos suffered from lack of food and water, making them weaker and more vulnerable to poachers. The colonial British government maintained a population in the Chitwan Royal Hunting Preserve in Nepal, and took measures to protect the rhinos, creating more reserves and sanctuaries to secure land and animals. In 1908 they set aside the Kaziranga area of Assam, India, as a forest reserve, designating it a wildlife sanctuary in 1916.[23]

The scarcity of the rhinoceros shot horn prices ever upward and by the 1930s troops had to be deployed to guard the protected rhinos from poachers. After Indian independence Assam led the way in wildlife conservation. By 1956 the International Union for Conservation took the Indian rhino off its 'Fossils of Tomorrow' list, though at the time one biologist claimed, 'we know little more now about its ecology than did Marco Polo in 1298.'[24]

Although the Indian rhinoceros remains on the endangered species list, it is one of the greatest success stories in the history of conservation – and certainly the biggest boon in efforts to save Asian rhinos. Native to Nepal and Assam, this rhino once roamed from Pakistan to Burma, perhaps even as far as Myanmar and China. Human settlement reduced its range, encroached on its habitat and pushed it to its current home of tall grasslands and riverine forests in the foothills of the Himalayas.

With a semi-prehensile upper lip it grazes on grasses, leaves and aquatic plants and fruits, and is a good swimmer. Its thick silver-brown skin falls into huge folds, its upper legs and shoulders are often covered with wart-like bumps. Sometimes called the great one-horned, or Asian one-horned, rhinoceros, it is, along with Africa's white rhino, the fourth largest land animal in the world, falling just behind the three species of elephant. It can weigh between 1,800 and 2,700 kg, stands 1.75–2 metres tall, and measures 3–3.8 metres long. Its impressive single horn, the inspiration for so many myths, ranges from 20 to 61 cm high.

The Indian rhinoceros is more amphibious than other species, enjoys grazing on aquatic grasses while wading through riverine grasslands and is even capable of diving to reach underwater sources of food. They give birth in quicker intervals than most, with a calf coming as frequently as one to three years. Cows reach sexual maturity at five to seven years of age, and gestation is the same sixteen months as it is for other rhinos. Again, the males mature later, as late as ten years old. Life expectancy is 35–45 years in the wild, and about the same in captivity. Indian rhinos of both sexes are solitary, except for mothers and infants, and inhabit specific territories. Females are greatly tolerant of intruders and overlapping ranges, but males battle violently for their territory, resulting often in the death of one badly wounded rhino.

Along with habitat loss, poaching reduced the numbers of the Indian rhinoceros to only 200 individuals in the early

Indian rhinoceros.

twentieth century. With protection from Indian and Nepalese governments, and efforts by conservation groups, poaching was regulated and habitat protected within the confines of Kaziranga National Park and Manas National Park, both in Assam, and the Royal Chitwan National Park in Nepal. Although it took nearly 80 years to surpass the 1,000 mark, since 1983 Indian rhino numbers have more than doubled to 2,500 individuals.

The Indian rhinoceros is Asia's only story of conservation success thus far. Although poaching continues and the Indian rhinoceros has disappeared from a few areas where it formerly lived. Not only do populations need to be saved and expanded in situ but, to preserve the integrity of the species and to prevent complete wipe out from a natural disaster or disease, rhino populations need to exist in diverse locales. In 2003 the World Wide Fund for Nature (WWF) relocated a group of ten Indian rhinos from their primary protected range at Royal Chitwan National Park to a new habitat at Royal Bardia National Park.[25]

Because previous population counts for the Indian rhinoceros rebounded from numbers which were as low as current counts

Ecotourists observe a rhinoceros while riding elephants.

for its continental subspecies, many retain hope for the Javan and Sumatran to follow in the footsteps of its larger relation.

JAVAN RHINOCEROS

An astonishingly low estimate of 60 Javan rhinoceroses (*Rhinoceros sondaicus*) reside in their primary habitat, the Ujung Kulon National Park in Java. An even smaller population, probably fewer than fifteen rhinos, lives in the Cat Loc Nature Reserve in Vietnam. In the mid-nineteenth century there were three subspecies of the Javan rhinoceros, of which *sondaicus*, or Indonesian, is the only significant member left. *Inermis* and *annamiticus* are thought to be extinct. The scarcity of the remaining subspecies has earned it the dubious title of 'the rarest large mammal in the world'.

Often referred to as the Asian lesser one-horned rhinoceros, the Javan rhino is significantly smaller than the Indian rhino, but larger than its other Asian relative, the Sumatran. They weigh in at 900–2,300 kg, average 1.5–1.7 metres tall and 2.0–4 metres long. A single horn rises at least 25 cm in males of the species. Its grey, hairless hide creases into folds, but these are less apparent than those of the Indian rhinoceros.

Javan rhinos prefer lowland tropical forests to the open grasslands favoured by other rhinos. Living solitary lives in this region, Javan rhinos are pure browsers. When they inhabited lowland waterways, however, they probably mixed browsing and grazing. Despite their rarity they seem quite adaptable to new food sources. Birthing, sexual maturity and life expectancy are assumed to be about the same as Indian rhinos, but with so few in existence true figures are difficult to reach. Although they do not defend their territory, if threatened their sharp lower teeth are an effective method of attack, as they are for all Asian rhinos. Their horns are used primarily for deepening wallows and protection when breaking through forested areas.

Javan rhinoceros.

The small number of Javan rhinoceroses and their isolated habitat put it in grave danger of extinction. Unlike larger rhinos, Javan live shorter lives in captivity than in the wild. The few which have been kept have survived only 22 years – at least ten years shorter than in the wild. Even with successful protection in parks, their numbers only slightly more than doubled from 25 to 60 between 1967 and 1984. An unidentified disease threatened the population of Ujung Kulon National Park in the early 1980s, killing five individuals. Poachers could quickly wipe out the species and, with none kept in captivity and no breeding programmes, the Javan rhinoceros would not only be extinct in the wild, but disappear from the earth for good. As if this wasn't enough danger, their primary home on the Ujung Kulon peninsula sits in the path of volcanic activity which could rain ash or flood with tidal waves at any moment.[26]

Survival is a game of chance for the Javan rhinoceros.

SUMATRAN RHINOCEROS

The closest relative to the prehistoric ancestor, the woolly rhinoceros, the Sumatran rhinoceros (*Dicerorhinus sumatrensis*) retains specks of hair reminiscent of the ancient's lustrous coat. Frequently dubbed the hairy rhino, its reddish-brown hair allows it to live at cool, high altitudes in the mountains of Borneo and Sumatra. It is the smallest of the five rhino groups, standing at an average of 1–1.5 metres tall and 2–3 metres long and weighing only 600–950 kg. The Sumatran is the only two-horned rhino in Asia; its front protrusion measures 25–79 cm, the secondary one stands at only 10 cm.

Like the Javan rhinoceros, the Sumatran inhabit tropical forest but remain in both lowland and highland ranges. Maturity is the same as other Asian species and females give birth every three years, with sixteen-month pregnancies.

Sumatran
rhinoceros.

Generally solitary, they browse the diverse vegetation of dense forests for an average of 35 years of life. The main centres of limited social activity are salt licks, which add important minerals to their diet. Trails cut through the forest by rhinos and other animals often lead to such places where poachers find a predictable arena for traps. They are quick and nimble, able to break through tangles of rainforest, run up steep slopes and climb forested mountains.

Since the 1960s the countryside outside of Kuala Lumpur has been deforested for the timber industry, covered with rubber plantations and dredged for tin mines. What forest cover did remain was frequently traversed by humans tapping trees for the latex used in chewing gum. Sumatran rhinos cling to life at the Bukit Belata Forest Reserve, just a hundred miles from the city, 'on a kind of island bounded by swamps and human beings'.[27]

Designated by IUCN as Critically Endangered, the Sumatran rhinoceros faces the same threats as its relatives. Its prehensile lip is used for grazing the lowland secondary rainforest, swamps and moss forests. This flexible diet allows it to live in isolated mountain forests where shrubs and vines are plentiful. Traditionally, they only moved to higher altitudes during the rainy season, but with human encroachment they are now forced further up the mountains year round. Because they live at higher elevations and in denser forests, Sumatran rhinoceroses have fared a bit better than the Javan. This locale kept habitat loss at bay; logging and human settlement came much slower. Over the last decade, however, numbers have fallen by 50 per cent.

Lydekker's sketch of a Sumatran rhinoceros.

The most populous of the three subspecies is the western (*D. s. sumatrensis*) which lives in Sumatra. The last count was 300 individuals roaming the inaccessible mountains of Sundaland in Southeast Asia in small and fragmented populations, where the Indonesian government has not outlawed clear cutting for timber. At last count there were only 50 eastern (*D. s. harrissoni*) in Sabah and Borneo and unconfirmed sightings in Sarawak and Kalimantan. The Indian and Bangladesh native, the northern Sumatran rhinoceros (*D. s. lasiotis*), is believed extinct, though some maintain there remain a few in Myanmar (Burma).

In a tragic irony, the rarity of the Sumatran rhino has caused more poaching. Banking on its extinction, dealers stock up on the horn, already worth $200 per gram, knowing prices will increase upon its complete disappearance. On Sumatra their widespread habitat over the island nation makes protection difficult, though an international effort supported by the United Nations Development Programme is attempting to prevent poaching.

Captive breeding programmes have met with mixed success. Between 1984 and 1995 forty rhinos were taken, but half of them died. Only one calf was born – and that one was not bred in captivity. Only a few Sumatran rhinos live in captivity where breeding has met with much difficulty and there is little hope for reintroduction into the wild. One infant was born at the Cincinnati Zoo on 30 July 2004 and another on 1 May 2007.[28]

A NEW IMAGE?

After hearing so many stories about rhinoceroses, I sat down with Dr Pat Thomas, Curator of Mammals at the Wildlife Conservation Society. Here I was, once again, trying to figure out the nature of a wild beast surrounded by the asphalt of New York City. On the upper floor of a red-brick and stone building, in the historic centre of the Bronx Zoo, Dr Thomas's office seemed about as far from a wild animal as one could get. Ernest Thompson Seton drawings hung on the wall, figurines of horses and two rhinoceros statues stood alertly on top of the bookshelf behind his desk.

The Bronx Zoo has been the most successful American zoological park at breeding Indian rhinoceroses. When I met with Dr Thomas in March of 2007, he showed me photographs of two new calves, one female and one male. They looked much like their adult counterparts, their skin already looked heavy and thickly plated, but between the grey folds were bright pink crevasses. Of course they had no horns yet, but Dr Thomas pointed out the bump on the forefront of the snout where it would start to grow.

The Bronx Zoo's Sumatran rhinoceros.

Although Dr Thomas said the zoo does not like to publicize the names of its animals, a recent rhinoceros in its collection possessed a highly symbolic name. Rapunzel was a Sumatran rhinoceros, and among some grizzly bears and Asian elephants, one of the zoo's few wild-born animals. She was rescued from a rainforest about to be cleared for a palm tree plantation in Sumatra, and brought (along with three others) to the Cincinnati Zoo. This rescue was part of a joint attempt by American zoos and the Indonesian government called the Sumatran Rhino Trust, which seeks to breed the rhinos in captivity in hopes of someday releasing them to a safer wilderness than they now inhabit.[29]

Because of the scarcity of rhinos, each one remaining becomes symbolic. While the first captive rhinos served as proof of the existence of such creatures, Rapunzel's captive existence was a poignant reminder of the very absence of the species in the wild. Attempts to mate her failed, and from Cincinnati she went to the Bronx Zoo, where she inhabited the old Elephant House until she died in 2005.

The story of Rapunzel is a tale of a princess, locked in a tower and saved by a prince who climbs her long hair. In yet another turn of mythology Rapunzel forces us to imagine the rhino as the princess – safely locked away – but not free. Yet it is only in such confinement that her existence could be ensured. With no mate to climb her impossibly short hair, Rapunzel died without an heir. Her body was sent to the American Museum of Natural History where it will probably stand someday as a relic – just as people have predicted and imagined for centuries – of a prehistoric, even mythic age, when nature was more powerful than humanity.

Timeline of the Rhinoceros

30,000 BC	8000 BC	2000 BC	2000 BC	275–274 BC
Ancient humans paint rhinoceros images in Chauvet Cave, France	Woolly rhinoceros becomes extinct	Chinese hunt rhinoceros and use hide for armour	Rhinoceros imagery appears on Indus Valley seals	Ptolemy II Philadelphus parades white rhinoceros through Alexandria

1749	1822	1830	1850	1854
Jean-Baptiste Oudry's life-size painting of Clara the rhino	Campbell's rhinoceros/unicorn skull reaches Europe	First living rhinoceros arrives in America Featherstonehaugh finds fossil rhino jaw in Pennsylvania	Cumming's battle with his 'hideous monster' appears in print	B. W. Hawkins displays Iguanodon sculpture at the 'dinosaur park' at Crystal Palace, Sydenham, Kent

1934	1937	1950	1955	1960s
Fictional war of Babar the Elephant and Rataxes the Rhinoceros	Katherine Lane Weems unveils her sculptures of Bessie	Dalí claims a rhinoceros horn will save his life	Disney's *Jungle Cruise* immortalizes charging rhinoceros	Tranquillizers used to relocate African rhinos

55 BC	AD 77	c. 1300	1515	1577–1603
Pompey stages rhino fights in Circus Maximus, Rome	Pliny writes of elephant–rhino animosity	Marco Polo reports unicorns in China	King Manuel stages anticlimactic rhino–elephant duel. Dürer sketches his *Rhinoceros*	Philip II of Portugal exhibits a rhinoceros alongside an elephant

1864	1902	1906	1908	1910
First rhino photo taken in London Zoo by Frank Haes	Rudyard Kipling explains why the rhino's skin is baggy	Baby black rhino Bessie is most expensive animal yet acquired by Bronx Zoo	Eye surgery performed on Mogul, an Indian rhinoceros in the Bronx Zoo	Roosevelt and Lang search for nearly extinct white rhinos in northern Africa; Lang bags two record-setting white rhino specimens

1970s	1977	1994	2005
Increase in demand for jambiyas	CITES bans trade in rhino horn	USA passes Tiger and Rhinoceros Conservation Act	Rapunzel dies at Bronx Zoo

References

1 ANCIENT AND MYTHIC

1 Edward R. Ricciuti, 'Perspective: the disappearing rhino', *Animal Kingdom*, LXXXIII/1 (1980), p. 57.
2 Marco Polo, *The Travels of Marco Polo* (New York, 2005).
3 Jean-Charles Seigneuret, *Dictionary of Literary Themes and Motifs* (Westport, CT, 1988).
4 Glynis Ridley, *Clara's Grand Tour: Travels with a Rhinoceros in Eighteenth-Century Europe* (New York, 2004), pp. 35–7.
5 Francis A. Ewing, MD, 'Bible Natural History; or a Description of the Animals, Plants, and Minerals, mentioned in the Sacred Scriptures, with copious references and explanations of Texts', *Princeton Review* (October 1835), pp. 559–73; 'True Unicorn, an inhabitant of Thibet', *Athenaeum; or, Spirit of the English Magazines*, IX/1 (1 April 1821), p. 41; 'The Unicorn', *Christian Review*, 21 (January 1856), p. 37.
6 'The Unicorn', *Weekly Recorder*, VII/28 (14 March 1821), p. 223.
7 'The Unicorn', *Ohio Miscellaneous Museum*, I/5 (May 1822), pp. 220–22.
8 Ridley, *Clara's Grand Tour*, p. 38; Seigneuret, *Dictionary of Literary Themes*; Anonymous, 'A Description of the Rhinoceros' (London, 1684), Folger Shakespeare Library Online Collection, www.rhino-resourcecenter.com/ref_files/1175830960.pdf; Conrad Gesner, *History of Four-Footed Beasts* (London, 1607).
9 'Unicorn', *Boston Medical Intelligencer*, III/13 (9 August 1825), p. 56.

10 'The Unicorn', *New-York Mirror*, XVI/12 (15 September 1838), p. 91.
11 Louis Agassiz, 'The System in Zoology', paper presented at the American Association for the Advancement of Science, 15 August 1855, p. 54.
12 W.J.T. Mitchell, *The Last Dinosaur Book* (Chicago, IL, and London, 1998).
13 Stephen Jay Gould, *I Have Landed: the End of a Beginning in Natural History* (New York, 2003).
14 Mitchell, *The Last Dinosaur Book*, p. 67.
15 Herbert Lang, 'The White Rhinoceros of the Belgian Congo', *Zoological Society Bulletin*, XXIII/4 (July 1920); Theodore Roosevelt, *African Game Trails: An Account of the African Wanderings of an American Hunter–Naturalist* (New York, 1988), pp. 206–8.
16 Paul Semonin, *American Monster: How the Nation's First Prehistoric Creature Became a Symbol of National Identity* (New York and London, 2000).
17 G. W. Featherstonehaugh, 'Rhinoceroides Alleghaniensis', *Monthly American Journal of Geology and Natural Science*, 1 (July 1831), p. 1.
18 *Casket*, 6 (June 1830), p. 278; *Saturday Evening Post*, IX/461 (29 May 1830); *Saturday Evening Post*, IX/478 (September 1830); *The Rose Bud, or Youth's Gazette*, 1/19 (5 January 1833), p. 76; *The Rose Bud, or Youth's Gazette*, 1/18 (29 December 1832), p. 72.

2 RHINOS ON THE ROAD

1 Phoebe George Bradford, 'Diary of Phoebe George Bradford, January, 1834', *Phoebe George Bradford Diaries* (Delaware, 1975), p. 86. Online at North American Women's Letters and Diaries, www.lib.uchicago.edu/efts/asp/NAWLD
2 Marina Belozerskaya, *The Medici Giraffe and Other Tales of Exotic Animals and Power* (New York, 2006).
3 Pliny the Elder, *Natural History* (New York, 1991).
4 Nancy Hathaway, *The Unicorn* (New York, 2005), pp. 54–5.
5 Belozerskaya, *The Medici Giraffe*, p. 81.
6 Glynis Ridley, *Clara's Grand Tour: Travels with a Rhinoceros in*

Eighteenth-Century Europe (New York, 2004), pp. 3, 85; Belozerskaya, *The Medici Giraffe*.

7 David Quammen, *The Boilerplate Rhino: Nature in the Eye of the Beholder* (New York, 2001); T. H. Clarke, *The Rhinoceros from Durer to Stubbs: 1515–1799* (London, 1986); Ridley, *Clara's Grand Tour*.

8 Anonymous, 'A Description of the Rhinoceros' (London, 1684). Online at Folger Shakespeare Library, www.rhinoresources-center.com/ref_files/1175830960.pdf

9 Ridley, *Clara's Grand Tour*, p. xvii.

10 *Ibid.*, pp. 24, 34.

11 *Ibid.*, pp. 73, 98–9.

12 Louise E. Robbins, *Elephant Slaves and Pampered Parrots: Exotic Animals in Eighteenth-Century Paris* (Baltimore, MD, 2002), pp. 93–7; Ridley, *Clara's Grand Tour*, p. 151.

13 Ridley, *Clara's Grand Tour*, pp. 43, 67–8.

14 *Ibid.*, pp. 55, 122.

15 *Ibid.*, p. 160.

16 Lee M. Talbot, 'Marco Polo's Unicorn', *Natural History*, LXVIII/10 (December 1959), p. 560.

17 David Carlyon, *Dan Rice: The Most Famous Man You've Never Heard Of* (New York, 2001), pp. 227–8.

18 *Saturday Evening Post*, IX/478 (September 1830).

19 *Ibid.*; 'Natural History: The One Horned Rhinoceros of India', *Mechanics' & Farmers' Magazine of Useful Knowledge* (15 July 1830).

20 'Natural History: The One Horned Rhinoceros of India'.

21 *Appleton's Journal: A Magazine of General Literature* (26 July 1873), p. 118.

22 George Augustus Sala, *Gaslight and Daylight*, pp. 195–7. Online at Victorian London, www.victorianlondon.org/publications2/gaslight-18.htm

23 Elwin R. Sanborn, 'The New Rhinoceros', *Zoological Society Bulletin*, I/22 (1906).

24 Herbert Lang, 'The White Rhinoceros of the Belgian Congo', *Zoological Society Bulletin*, XXIII/4 (July 1920).

25 Raymond L. Ditmars and William Bridges, *Wild Animal World:*

Behind the Scenes at the Zoo (New York and London, 1937), p. 41.

26 Sanborn, 'Death of the Indian Rhinoceros', *Zoological Society Bulletin*, XXI/5 (1918).

27 William Temple Hornaday, *A Wild Animal Round-Up* (New York and London, 1925), pp. 361–2.

28 Hornaday, 'The Elephant House', *Zoological Society Bulletin*, III/31 (October 1908).

29 Hornaday, 'The Elephant House', p. 451; Raymond Ditmars, 'Items of Interest', *Zoological Society Bulletin*, XXVIII/4 (1915), p. 1256.

30 William Temple Hornaday, *The Minds and Manners of Wild Animals: A Book of Personal Observations* (New York, 1922), p. 23.

31 Dick Richards, *Life with Alice: 40 Years of Elephant Adventures* (New York, 1944), p. 66.

32 *New York Zoological Society Annual Report for 1924*; Buck to Hornaday (30 March 1923), Wildlife Conservation Society Archives, the Bronx, New York.

33 Benson to Hornaday (14 February and 21 March 1923); Hornaday to Buck (5 May 1924), Wildlife Conservation Society Archives.

34 Louise Todd Ambler, *Katherine Lane Weems: Sculpture and Drawings* (Boston, MA, 1987).

35 Sam Dunton, 'Lights! Camera! Animals!', *Animal Kingdom*, LXXVII/5 (October/November 1974), p. 29; Dunton, 'Mid-Summer in the Zoo', in *Animal Kingdom*, LVIII/3 (June 1955).

36 Dunton, 'Lights! Camera! Animals!', p. 29.

37 Edalee Harwell, 'Animals in and Out of Africa', *Zoonooz*, LXII/2 (February 1989), pp. 6–7.

38 Melody Malmberg, *The Making of Disney's Animal Kingdom Theme Park* (New York, 1998), p. 138.

3 NATIVE HAUNTS

1 Ernest Hemingway, *Green Hills of Africa* (New York, 1963), p. 104.

2 Herbert Lang, 'The White Rhinoceros of the Belgian Congo', *Zoological Society Bulletin*, XXIII/4 (July 1920).

3 William Temple Hornaday, *The Minds and Manners of Wild Animals: A Book of Personal Observations* (New York, 1922).

4 'The Unicorn', *New-York Mirror*, xvi/12 (15 September 1838).

5 R. Gordon Cumming, *A Hunter's Life in South Africa*, 1 (London, 1850), p. 249.

6 *Ibid.*, n. 1, pp. 249–51.

7 *Ibid.*, pp. 294–5.

8 Theodore Roosevelt, *African Game Trails: An Account of the African Wanderings of an American Hunter–Naturalist* (New York, 1988), pp. 67, 106, 138–41.

9 Hornaday, *The Minds and Manners of Wild Animals*, pp. 23, 158; Lang, 'The White Rhinoceros'.

10 Roosevelt, *African Game Trails*, pp. 105, 141, 212.

11 Hemingway, *Green Hills of Africa*, pp. 86–7.

12 *Ibid.*, pp. 79, 83–93.

13 Lang, 'The White Rhinoceros'.

14 Hornaday, 'National Collection of Heads and Horns', *Zoological Society Bulletin*, 40 (July 1910).

15 Hornaday, 'Our White Rhinoceros Head', *Zoological Society Bulletin*, 46 (1911); Hornaday, 'National Collection'.

16 Hornaday, 'American Taxidermy' (unpubd source book), p. 306, Wildlife Conservation Society Archives, the Bronx, New York.

17 James L. Clark, 'The work of the department of preparation' (20 October 1929), in *Radio Talks by J.L.C. 1927–1933*, unpublished archival material, American Museum of Natural History Rare Books Collection.

18 James L. Clark, 'Field Sketch-book on his First African Trip 1908–09–10', unpublished archival material, American Museum of Natural History Rare Books Collection.

19 Clark, 'The work of the department of preparation', *Radio Talks*.

20 *Ibid.*

21 Press Release (2 January 1938), American Museum of Natural History, New York, Central Archives, cat. no. 1178.4.

22 Davison to Mary Akeley (15 December 1936), American Museum of Natural History, Central Archives.

23 'An Unfinished Exhibit', *New York Herald Tribune* (26 February 1937); John H. Bennett, 'In Memory of Carl Akeley', *New York Herald Tribune* (27 March 1937); Davison to Leeds (telegram, 14 January 1941), American Museum of Natural History, Central Archives; Butler to Andrews (7 September 1937), American Museum of Natural History, Central Archives.

24 Redmond O'Hanlon, *Into the Heart of Borneo* (New York, 1984), pp. 61, 127, 135, 183.

4 CULTURAL LIFE

1 Herbert Lang, 'The White Rhinoceros of the Belgian Congo', *Zoological Society Bulletin*, xxiii/4 (July 1920).

2 *How Giraffe Got Such a Long Neck . . . And Why Rhino is so Grumpy*, retold by Michael Rosen (New York, 1993); 'Why the Giraffe has a Long Neck', in *When Hippo was Hairy: and other Tales from Africa*, told by Nick Greaves, illustrated by Rod Clement (Auckland, 1988), pp. 86–8.

3 Jean de Brunhoff, *Babar and The Travels of Babar* (New York, 1961).

4 Roald Dahl, *James and the Giant Peach* (New York, 1961).

5 Greaves, 'Why Rhino scatters his Dung', in *When Hippo was Hairy*, pp. 60–64.

6 *The Rumor: A Jataka Tale from India*, retold and illustrated by Jan Thornhill (Ontario, 2002); 'The End of the World', in *Twenty Jataka Tales*, retold by Noor Inayat Khan, illustrated by H. Willebeek Le Mair (Rochester, vt, 1985), pp. 125–32.

7 Rudyard Kipling, 'How the Rhinoceros got his Skin', in *Just So Stories* (Harmondsworth, 1987), pp. 27–36.

8 Floyd Norman, *Jim Hill Media*, blog (19 September 2006), online at www.jimhillmedia.com (accessed 29 October 2007).

9 Shel Silverstein, *Who Wants a Cheap Rhinoceros* (New York, 1964).

10 Frank Haes quoted by Kenneth Baker, 'Stanford show captures early photographers trying to freeze a moment', *San Francisco Chronicle* (28 April 2003).

11 Ian Gibson, *The Shameful Life of Salvador Dalí* (New York, 1998), p. 531–2; Ralf Schiebler, *Dalí: The Reality of Dreams* (New York, 2005).

12 James Mackay, *The Animaliers: a Collector's Guide to the Animal Sculptors of the 19th & 20th Centuries* (New York, 1973); Christopher Payne, *Animals in Bronze* (Suffolk, 1986).

13 Hergé, *TinTin in the Congo* (London, 2006), p. 56.

14 Ernest Hemingway, *Green Hills of Africa* (New York, 1963); Lang, 'The White Rhinoceros'.

15 'None Tougher', *Saturday Evening Post* (25 August 1951), p. 27.

16 Marc Ecko Enterprises, 'June 8th Event to Support the World's Dwindling Rhino Populations', Press Release (4 May 2006).

5 HORNS, HABITS AND HABITATS

1 Lee M. Talbot, 'Marco Polo's Unicorn', *Natural History*, LXVIII/10 (December 1959), p. 563.

2 Herbert Lang, 'The White Rhinoceros of the Belgian Congo', *Zoological Society Bulletin*, XXIII/4 (July 1920).

3 Richard Ellis, *Tiger Bone & Rhino Horn: The Destruction of Wildlife for Traditional Chinese Medicine* (Washington, DC, 2005); Esmond Bradley Martin, *Run Rhino Run* (London, 1982); Eric Dinerstein, *Return of the Unicorns: Natural History and Conservation of the Greater One-Horned Rhinoceros* (New York, 2003).

4 Ellis, *Tiger Bone*.

5 *Ibid*.

6 Martin, 'The Conspicuous Consumption of Rhinos', *Animal Kingdom*, LXXXI/1 (1981).

7 Edward R. Riciutti, 'Perspective: the disappearing rhino', *Animal Kingdom*, LXXXIII/1 (1980); Ellis, *Tiger Bone*.

8 Catherine Clyne interview with Patrick Brown, 'Black Market: Exposing Asia's Illegal Animal Trade', *Satya* (May 2005); Ben Davies, *Black Market: Inside the Endangered Species Trade in Asia* (California, 2005).

9 Martin, 'The Conspicuous Consumption'.

10 Clyne, 'Black Market'.

11 Clyne, 'Black Market'; Talbot, 'Marco Polo's Unicorn'.

12 Frants Hartmann, 'Saving the African Rhino', *Animal Kingdom*
LXXVI/1 (1973), p. 104.

13 Riciutti, 'Perspective'.

14 Andrew Laurie, 'Stumptail and Company', *Animal Kingdom*,
LXXIX/4 (1976).

15 International Rhino Foundation, online at www.rhinos-irf.org/
rhinoinformation/whiterhino/index.htm (accessed 29 October
2007).

16 Hartmann 'Saving the African Rhino'; International Rhino
Foundation, online at www.rhinos-irf.org/rhinoinformation/
blackrhino/index.htm (accessed 29 October 2007); R. Emslie and
M. Brooks, eds, *African Rhino. Status Survey and Conservation
Action Plan* (Cambridge, 1999).

17 N. J. Russell, 'Rhinos, Whirlybirds and M99', *Animal Kingdom*,
LXX/4 (1967).

18 C.A.W. Guggisberg, 'An Appreciation of African Rhinoceroses',
Animal Kingdom, LXVII/4 (August 1964).

19 Edalee Harwell, 'Animals in and Out of Africa', *Zoonooz*, LXII/2
(February 1989).

20 Guggisberg, 'An Appreciation'.

21 *Ibid.*

22 *Ibid.*

23 Talbot, 'Marco Polo's Unicorn'.

24 *Ibid.*, p. 564.

25 International Rhino Foundation, online at www.rhinos-
irf.org/rhinoinformation/indianrhino/index.htm (accessed 29
October 2007).

26 Thomas J. Foose and Nico van Strien, eds, *Asian Rhinos – Status
Survey and Conservation Action Plan* (Cambridge, 1997).

27 Oliver Milton, 'Rubber, Tin—and Rhinos', *Animal Kingdom*,
LXV/2 (April 1962).

28 International Rhino Foundation, online at www.rhinos-
irf.org/rhinoinformation/sumatranrhino/index.htm (accessed 29

October 2007).

29 Author interview with Dr Patrick Thomas, Curator of Mammals, Wildlife Conservation Society (March 2007); Andy Newman, 'Rapunzel the Rhino is Mourned in Bronx', *New York Times*, 24 December 2005; 'At Bronx Zoo, a Damsel in Distress is Rescued', *New York Times*, 7 June 1990.

Bibliography

Balfour, Daryl and Sharna, *Rhino: The Story of the Rhinoceros and a Plea for its Conservation* (Cape Town, 1991)

Belozerskaya, Marina, *The Medici Giraffe: And Other Tales of Exotic Animals and Power* (New York, 2006)

Booth, Martin, *Rhino Road: The Black and White Rhinos of Africa* (London, 1992)

Clarke, T. H., *The Rhinoceros from Dürer to Stubbs: 1515–1799* (London, 1986)

Cumming, R. Gordon, *A Hunter's Life in South Africa*, vol. I (London, 1850)

Cunningham, Carol and Joel Berger, *Horn of Darkness: Rhinos on the Edge* (New York, 1997)

Dinerstein, Eric, *Return of the Unicorns: Natural History and Conservation of the Greater One-Horned Rhinoceros* (New York, 2003)

Ditmars, Raymond L. and William Bridges, *Wild Animal World: Behind the Scenes at the Zoo* (New York and London, 1937)

Ellis, Richard, *Tiger Bone & Rhino Horn: The Destruction of Wildlife for Traditional Chinese Medicine* (Washington, DC, 2005)

Guggisberg, C.A.W., *s.o.s. Rhino* (New York, 1966)

Hanson, Elizabeth, *Animal Attractions: Nature on Display in American Zoos* (Princeton, NJ, 2002)

Hathaway, Nancy, *The Unicorn* (New York, 2005)

Heller, Edmund, *The White Rhinoceros* (Washington, DC, 1913)

Hemingway, Ernest, *Green Hills of Africa* (New York, 1935)

Johnson, Osa, *I Married Adventure* (New York, 1940)

Martin, Esmond Bradley, *Run Rhino Run* (London, 1982)

Merz, Anna, *Rhino at the Brink of Extinction* (London, 1991)

Mitchell, W.J.T., *The Last Dinosaur Book* (Chicago, IL, and London, 1998)

Nardelli, Franceso, et al., *The Rhinoceros: A Monograph* (London, 1998)

Penny, Malcolm, *Rhinos: Endangered Species* (New York, 1988)

Player, Ian, *The White Rhino Saga* (New York, 1972)

Pliny the Elder, *Natural History* (New York, 1991)

Ridley, Glynis, *Clara's Grand Tour: Travels with a Rhinoceros in Eighteenth-Century Europe* (New York, 2004)

Robbins, Louise E., *Elephant Slaves and Pampered Parrots: Exotic Animals in Eighteenth-century Paris* (Baltimore, MD, 2002)

Rookmaaker, Leendert Cornelis, *Bibliography of the Rhinoceros: An Analysis of the Literature on the Recent Rhinoceroses in Culture, History and Biology* (Rotterdam, 1983)

Roosevelt, Theodore, *African Game Trails: An Account of the African Wanderings of an American Hunter-Naturalist* (New York, 1988)

Rothfels, Nigel, *Savages and Beasts: The Birth of the Modern Zoo* (Baltimore, MD, 2002)

Quammen, David, *The Boilerplate Rhino: Nature in the Eye of the Beholder* (New York, 2001)

Associations and Websites

RHINO RESOURCE CENTER
www.rhinoresourcecenter.org

SOS RHINO
www.sosrhino.org

SAVE THE RHINO INTERNATIONAL
www.savetherhino.org

INTERNATIONAL RHINO FOUNDATION
www.rhinos-irf.org

WORLD WILDLIFE FUND TRADITIONAL CHINESE MEDICINE UNIT
www.tcmwildlife.org

WILDLIFE CONSERVATION SOCIETY / BRONX ZOO
www.wcs.org

Pachyderm, Journal of IUCN (The World Conservation Union: http://iucn.org) African Elephant, African Rhino and Asian Rhino Specialist Groups: http://www.iucn.org/themes/ssc/sgs/afesg/pachy

Acknowledgements

Ann Fabian set off more than she knew when she told me about a mysterious man who imported a rhinoceros to America. From my original essay to drafts of this book, her guidance, discussions and editing have been outstanding. Most of all, I am appreciative for her curiosity for the curious which has justified my own odd academic endeavours.

At the Animals & History Conference in Cologne I met many welcoming scholars whose questions and comments challenged my thinking. For their insights during continued conversations, I especially thank Nigel Rothfels, Dorothee Brantz, and Brett Mizelle. It was here that I met the 'Animal' series editor Jonathan Burt, whose kindness encouraged this project. I am fortunate for the confidence he and publisher Michael Leaman placed in me to write this book.

I enjoyed the assistance of many archivists and librarians in my search for elusive rhinos: Jacqueline Borgenson at the Martin & Osa Johnson Safari Museum; and Barbara Mathe and Tom Baione at the American Museum of Natural History, and especially Steve Johnson at the Wildlife Conservation Society whose generosity has been invaluable. Johnny Fraser, Suzanne Bolduc, and Dr Patrick Thomas – also at WCS – have been equally generous with their time and assistance.

For their support, I thank my professors and colleagues at Rutgers University, especially Susan Schrepfer, Paul Clemens, T. J. Jackson Lears, Paul Israel, Neil Maher, Jan Lewis, Teresa Collins, Louis Carlat and Phil Scranton. The friendship of Karen Routledge, Ed Gitre and Alexandra Rimer has provided encouragement and sanity.

This book could not have been written without the comfort of friends and family. My heartfelt thanks goes to Jeffrey Enright and Kristen Giorgio, for *not* asking me about rhinos; Todd Parker, whose lofty goals inspired my own; Ben Johnson, for his calm companionship; and Wally, for her happiness. My parents have provided wonderful and constant support for this, and all my ambitious endeavours. To them I am eternally grateful.

Photo Acknowledgements

The author and publishers wish to express their thanks to the following sources of illustrative material and/or permission to reproduce it. Locations, etc., of some items are also given below.

Photos American Museum of Natural History, New York: pp. 8, 66 (Rare Books), 76, 81, 83, 85 (Photo Archives); American Periodical Series: p. 26; Archives of American Art, Washington, DC: p. 57; collection of the author: pp. 104, 116, 147, 149; Barnum Museum, Florida: pp. 6, 106; photo courtesy of The British Museum, London: p. 34; photos Disney Archives, Hollywood: pp. 95, 101, 102; Freer Gallery of Art, Smithsonian Institution, Washington, DC (gift of Charles Lang Freer, F1907.625): p. 13 (photo courtesy Freer Gallery of Art and Arthur M. Sackler Gallery, Smithsonian Insitution, Washington, DC); photo Getty Imaging Services: p. 82 (bottom left); photo Rustin Gudim: p. 132; photos Magnum Photos, New York: pp. 107, 115; photos Martin and Osa Johnson Safari Museum, Chanute, KS: pp. 61 (Stanton Collection), 67, 69, 82; 90, 91; photo The Metropolitan Museum of Art, New York: p. 24; Musée du Moyen Age, Cluny (photo R.G. Ojeda/Réunion des Musées Nationaux/Art Resource, New York): p. 13; photos Nature Photo Library: pp. 122, 123, 125, 138, 140, 142, 143, 146; photos New York Public Library: pp. 27, 109, 144 (Digital Collection); photo courtesy of Newberry Library, Chicago: p. 22; Photo Library/Oxford Images: p. 144; courtesy Random House, New York: p. 96; photos courtesy of the Rhino Resource Center/Klaus Bartholomess, London: pp. 18, 32, 41, 54; photo courtesy Richard

Redding Antiques, Ltd: p. 39; photos Karen Routledge: pp. 9, 146; photos Rutgers University Digital Services, New Brunswick, NJ: pp. 48, 64, 80, 92, 103, 104, 138; photo San Diego Zoological Society: p. 133; photo courtesy of US Fish and Wildlife Service: p. 136; Walters Art Gallery, Baltimore: p. 31; photo The Andy Warhol Museum, Pittsburg, PA (Photo courtesy the Artists Rights Society): p. 118; photos courtesy of Wildlife Conservation Society Archives, New York: pp. 43, 44, 46, 49, 73, 147; Wildlife Conservation Society Photo Collection, Bronx, NY: pp. 52, 54, 140; photo WWF Malaysia: p. 88.

Index